Parent to Parent

WLU Series

Whole Language Umbrella

The Whole Language Umbrella, an organization within the National Council of Teachers of English, is composed of language arts educators and others who view whole language as a dynamic philosophy of education. Through this series, WLU encourages discussion of critical issues within whole language, including promoting research and study of and disseminating information of whole language and facilitating collaboration among teachers, researchers, parents, administrators, and teacher educators.

Series Co-editors: David E. Freeman, Fresno Pacific College, and Yvonne S. Freeman, Fresno Pacific College

WLU Executive Board: Gerald R. Oglan, President, Wayne State University, Detroit; Stephen Hornstein, President-Elect, St. Cloud University, Minnesota; Kittye Copeland, Past-President, Vancouver, Washington; Judy Kelly, Secretary/Treasurer, Lincoln Elementary, Monroe, Michigan; Peggy Albers, Georgia State University, Atlanta; Amy Seely Flint, Language Education, Bloomington, Indiana; Barbara Bell, Western Carolina University, Cullowhee, North Carolina; Gail Heald-Taylor, University of Windsor, Ontario, Canada; Bobbi Jentes Mason, Fresno Pacific College, California; Carol Myers, Ashford, South Australia; Linda M. Cameron, University of Toronto, Canada; Robert C. Wortman, Elizabeth Borton Magnet Elementary, Tucson, Arizona; Brian Cambourne, University of Wollongong, Australia

Volumes in the Series

Beyond Reading and Writing: Inquiry, Curriculum, and Multiple Ways of Knowing (2000), Beth Berghoff, Kathryn A. Egawa, Jerome C. Harste, and Barry T. Hoonan

Parent to Parent: Our Children, Their Literacy (2001), Gerald R. Oglan and Averil Elcombe

Parent to Parent

OUR CHILDREN, THEIR LITERACY

Gerald R. Oglan
Wayne State University, Detroit, Michigan

Averil Elcombe
Heatherington Public School, Windsor, Ontario

 Whole Language Umbrella

National Council of Teachers of English
1111 W. Kenyon Road, Urbana, Illinois 61801–1096

Staff Editor: Rita D. Disroe

Interior Design: Pat Mayer

Cover Design: Tom Jaczak

Cover photo of father and child © Blair Seitz, Photo Researchers

Cover photo of mother and child by PhotoDisc

NCTE Stock Number: 34963-3050

Library of Congress Cataloging-in-Publication Data

Oglan, Gerald R., 1949–
    Parent to parent : our children, their literacy/Gerald R. Oglan, Averil Elcombe.
        p.   cm.
    Includes bibliographical references.
    ISBN 0-8141-3496-3
    1. Language arts (Early childhood) 2. Language arts (Elementary) 3. Early childhood education—Parent participation. 4. Education, Elementary—Parent participation. 5. Children—Books and reading. I. Elcombe, Averil, 1947– II. Title.

LB1139.5.L35 O45 2000
372.6—dc21   00-045233

We dedicate this book to our families:
Maureen, Nadia, and Jarrod
Jon, Kristin, Muffy, Alexis, and Greer

Contents

Foreword

You are holding in your hands an invitation to join your children on an exciting journey, one taken as they learn to read, write, listen, and speak—that is, as they become "literate." Our guides on this journey are Gerry and Averil, who, like all good guides, have prepared themselves by consulting the experts, in this case parents and children, for information and help in promoting the proficient and satisfying use of language. Our authors promise "to step back and let the voices of parents guide." There's a promise well kept. In fact, because Gerry and Averil consider you, too, a primary source of knowledge about your children, you are asked to join in the planning, doing, and celebrating of speaking, listening, reading, and writing that enrich children's lives.

Like good hosts, the authors' intention "is to provide . . . strategies . . . suggestions . . . and resources" to help even the most hesitant parents who want to help their children enjoy both oral and written language. Again, their intention is achieved. Gerry and Averil do not claim to give a *complete* list of activities to be strictly followed. Nor do they give a definitive catalog of books and tips to toss in a bag of literacy tricks. Rather, they suggest and show. They convey ideas by example and story, and through their stories and the stories of other parents, they encourage us to investigate more deeply into literacy learning and teaching. They do describe possible literacy-building experiences and provide rich references, but they remind us that the parent and the child are the ultimate decision makers.

Reflected in this book is great concern and care for all language learners and for the adults (parents, teachers, friends) in children's lives. If you fully accept the authors' invitation, you have awaiting you a "transactive experience," that is, an experience in which you are not only active in constructing meaning from the stories and examples shared, but one in which you also contribute to the process of creating the text. Each chapter begins with real questions, that is, questions actually asked by parents who have attended Gerry and Averil's workshops—questions that you might ask. As you read, you will gain information about children's growth as readers, writers, speakers, and listeners. There are stories about Gerry and Averil's children as well as stories from other parents. Such sharing is sure to remind you of a story about the children in your life. At the close of each chapter, you are invited to reflect and then to jot down your lingering thoughts about what you've read and pondered. These writings—creations—are a "planning point" for learning and growing with your own children.

If possible, enjoy this book with a spouse or friend; you'll want to talk about the suggestions given, the stories told, and your own unforgettable experiences.

Dorothy J. Watson
Professor Emeritus
University of Missouri–Columbia

Acknowledgments

No book about parents would be possible without the help and support of many individuals. This book originated from workshops we held for parent volunteers who were working with students in schools. In their role as parent volunteers, they read with children, helped them write and edit stories, or just sat and talked with them. Noticing the increasing numbers of parent volunteers, we decided to provide them with professional development.

The response from principals and parents was overwhelming. In our workshops, we modeled and demonstrated reading and writing strategies, had parents try the strategies, and then discussed how parents might use them with children. One parent responded this way on her evaluation sheet: "I wish I had this information when my children were growing up, I could have helped them a lot more instead of standing by feeling helpless." We decided that if one parent felt this way, then there must be others, so we conducted evening workshops at schools, and once again, the response was positive. Based on these experiences, we decided that we could reach out to more parents if we put our workshops into a book.

We are grateful to all of the parents from Windsor, Ontario, and from Detroit who contributed stories, writing samples, photos, and suggestions to this book. In particular, in Windsor, we thank Sue Silver of Roseville Public School and Manon Macroix of Taylor Public School, and in Detroit, Sharon Murphy. We would also like to acknowledge all of the schools and parents in the Greater Essex County Public School board as well as the parents at the Literacy Center at Wayne State University in Detroit for all of their support.

While writing this book, we often exchanged family stories about our own children as well as our experiences growing up. We had an opportunity of moving in and out of our roles as parents and children. Our parents had so much to do with who we are as adults. We would like to thank Helen and Victor Oglan and Mary and Philip Horton for being our first teachers. And of course we also thank our families and children, who were patient and understanding during the writing of this book: Maureen, Nadia, Jarrod, Jon, Kristin, Muffy, Alexis, and Greer.

Permissions

Introduction

A Book for Parents?

This book resulted from workshops we conducted for parents who were interested in knowing how they could help children develop as readers and writers. Initially, we focused on parents who volunteer in classrooms. After meeting with these parents, the need to share this information with other parents became evident. Parent volunteers told us they were often approached by other parents who wanted to learn more about the developmental nature of learning to read, write, and spell. As word of our workshops spread, we soon found ourselves being asked by schools and parent groups to speak in their districts, too. We learned a great deal and discovered how eager parents were to learn about their children's literacy development.

We present this information to help you understand how children learn—how they develop as readers, writers, and spellers. We feature stories that parents share with regards to the strategies they tried at home with their children. Some stories are about babies and preschool children and how parents wanted them to love books and reading. Others concern teenagers and how parents felt a desire to help them develop a more positive attitude toward reading. Parents like you— parents who attended workshops and then had the courage to try at home with their children some of the ideas we presented—wrote the stories. These parents eagerly share what they learned and how they continue to use this information as they work with their children at home.

We wrote this book with you in mind. As both educators and parents, we want to let the words of the parents who taught us so much be the focus of this book. Wherever possible, we offer brief explanations so that you will understand how and why parents use these strategies. By presenting strategies other parents employ, we would like to step back and let the voices of other parents guide you through the book.

Parents As Learners

We hope that you will see yourself as a learner in this process. Research shows that whenever parents become involved in their children's learning, their children perform better in schools. Ralph Peterson (1992) believes parents bring life experiences and different ways of knowing to a learning situation, and it is important for parents to share their unique ways of knowing with their children. Research also shows that involvement should start at an early age and continue through adolescence. Janie Hydrick (1996) emphasizes that as parents we model attitudes toward the goals and purpose of learning that will lead to success in the twenty-first century. We invite you to share in these stories and use what you can to enhance your children's learning.

How the Book Is Set Up

Parents ask great questions. The workshops we conduct for parents are centered on questions from parents. As a result, each chapter begins with questions that parents have posed about reading, writing, speaking, listening, and spelling. These questions act as a starting point, a way to think about literacy development as it relates to the information in each chapter. We included a section at the end of each chapter for you to write your own "lingering thoughts" while they are fresh in your mind. You can use these notes as a starting point for your own learning. We hope these questions will serve as a source of discussion with other parents, teachers, and school officials. Through ongoing conversation, all members of the literacy community can work to enhance children's learning experiences. Each chapter concludes with a "Parent Story," written by parents who employed some of the strategies at home with their children. We follow the parent stories with descriptions of the strategies and how they can be used at home. These tips are meant to act as a starting point for you to begin. Strategies alone, however, are not enough; they must be supported by current research. Each chapter, therefore, provides you with a purpose for and meaning of the strategies suggested.

In Chapter 1, we examine speaking and listening skills from the time a child is born until she enters formal schooling. Research supports the connection between speaking and listening and reading and writing that parents often inquire about. In Chapter 2, we discuss reading development and describe strategies that readers use to develop reading comprehension, prior knowledge, and oral reading. In Chapter 3, we look at writing and spelling and how the two complement and support each other. Finally, in Chapter 4, we offer suggestions on how to begin working with your children. At the end of the book, we include an annotated bibliography of books that can be purchased for use at home. Many of these books were read and recommended by parents and can be found in local libraries, bookstores, or in your child's school. We also include a glossary of terms to help parents understand terms and meanings. Please note that throughout the book whenever we refer to a child we use he and she interchangeably. We did this knowing that while reading through the various chapters many of our readers would be thinking about their son, daughter, or perhaps both.

1 Listening and Speaking

- Why should you correct children's incorrect use of language?
- Do young children understand speech?
- Is there a relationship between speaking and listening?
- Why do schools now promote speaking/listening and reading/ writing together?

We start our workshops by providing parents with a template or context in which to think about reading and writing development. We like to draw similarities between learning to read and write and learning to speak and listen. This comparison is important because it sets the stage for understanding the developmental nature of learning and the role that parents play in this process.

Listening

From the time children are born and before they develop formal speech they are constantly hearing sounds in their environment. Most of the sounds they hear come from a mother or other primary caregiver. Few people, if any, question whether they should talk to babies (Hill, 1989). Long before infants can produce words, parents carry on conversations with them. These conversations appear one-sided and occur while the parent is engaged in some activity with the child—for example, changing, rocking, walking, carrying, singing, or feeding. In response, babies will look directly at the parent and move their heads to track a father's or mother's voice. Babies a few months old demonstrate their listening skills by looking, smiling, laughing, gesturing, and wiggling their arms and legs (Bredekamp & Copple, 1997). In doing so, they demonstrate their ability to communicate with their parents. As babies grow, they continue to develop listening skills by communicating with others in their environment.

The quality of language development depends on the skills children learn through listening and speaking, which in turn facilitate the development of reading and writing. Of these skills, listening and reading are receiving activities, while speaking and writing are producing activities. All four depend on one another. What we listen to and what we read form the language material from which we produce speech and writing. Listening is the first activity in our language to develop and probably takes up the most time (Penner & McConnell, 1977). Why are some people poor listeners? It is because from the time we are born, we think of listening as a passive rather than an active process. Good listening, however, is a highly active process that involves predicting, sampling, and confirming. Predicting encourages children to guess what they think a story might be about. Getting them to predict activates whatever information they have about the topic. Once children have made predictions, they sample the text by listening to the story. Sampling allows them to discuss what they predicted with what the text actually said. In doing so, they are able to confirm or reject many of their initial predictions. For instance, before you read a book, such as *Grandma's Secret*, by Paulette Bourgeois, look at the cover together with your children and ask them what they think the story might be about. Family stories such as this one make a good starting point because kids love to share episodes about their own grandparents (i.e., their prior knowledge) while they predict. As you read the story, pause briefly to confirm predictions and invite children to make more predictions. Some predictions will be discarded, while new predictions may emerge. Read through the story following the pattern of predicting, sampling text, confirming, rejecting, or making new predictions. In Chapters 2 and 3, we further discuss the three processes of predicting, sampling, and confirming in order to demonstrate their relationship to reading, writing, and spelling.

Speaking

C hildren develop speech patterns at different rates. Some young children develop the ability to speak very early, while others choose to say very little. As newborns, children make two types of sounds: crying and noncrying. Crying sounds usually indicate hunger, a need for a diaper change, discomfort after eating, or just fussiness. Noncrying sounds such as cooing, gurgles, sighs, and grunts indicate that the child is happy and satisfied. These early sounds were our child's attempt to communicate messages to us. Initially, new parents are often at a disadvantage because the sounds new babies make and the messages they carry are unfamiliar. Until they come to know the meaning of these messages, new parents rely on outside sources or voices of experience—parents, siblings, or friends—to help them understand their child's needs. Parents talk, sing, play music, and read to their children long before formal speaking is established. Researchers often refer to this form of teaching as a "demonstration." For example, as a young infant, the child vocalizes as a partner in a conversation. One partner talks, one listens; if one disengages, the other calls her back into the dialogue (Bredekamp & Copple, 1997).

By eight or nine months children begin to understand the meaning of certain words. Most of the words relate to their social world, which includes important adults, objects, and activities associated with their daily lives. Once most children reach eighteen months, they understand the meanings of many words and can comprehend sentences.

From two to three years of age, most children understand their native language and are quite talkative. They listen and ask the "why" question in order to engage adults. They also learn that words have power and relate to strong feelings ("Daddy come back"). They may use (including repetitions) as many as eleven to twelve thousand words in a day. By observing adults and siblings they begin to develop an awareness and importance of written language. They enjoy being read to and like to take part in the reading by pointing to objects and pictures and repeating words and phrases. At the age of four most children use around 15, 000 words in a day.

All of this is done without any formal instruction. Parents accomplish the goal of teaching their children about language through interpretation of early cries and sounds, and demonstration of language use in real situations. When children use a word incorrectly in a sentence, parents model and demonstrate the correct use through examples and discussions. For instance, if a child said, "Mommy goed to the store," we shouldn't "correct" him; instead, we should model the correct use of the verb by repeating, "Yes, you and Mommy went to the store." This way the child hears the correct usage in context and will internalize the usage. As a result of these experiences, children begin to construct their own knowledge about language long before they enter formal schooling.

Speaking and Listening: Learning from the Environment

Children learn to read the environment long before they read formal text. For instance, if you have ever traveled in a car with a child of three or four and had him spot two large yellow arches, he immediately says the word "McDonald's." The golden arches represent meaning for the child because he internalizes the symbol with his desire to eat and perhaps play at McDonald's. K-Mart was the second word Averil's daughter Kristin ever read. It was the second word for two reasons: first, it was often seen on a familiar family route in the neighborhood, and, second, Kristin's own name started with a "K." "Kristin" was the first word she read because it was important to her. Therefore, it was easy to talk about other signs and words that started with the letter "K." Gerry's son, Jarrod, loved to sit in the front seat of their van whenever they traveled to Florida so that he could read the signs along the way. At the time Jarrod was seven, and he loved to play the alphabet game (finding a sign that begins with each letter of the alphabet) using the road signs. Along with playing the game, Jarrod and his parents discussed the sounds and words on the signs. Since children learn a great deal about language from "environmental print," we suggest you take your children along to the grocery store, dentist office, department stores, and doctor's office. Along the way, have them "read" the environment. These types of language experiences help children develop an understanding of how oral and written language are used.

By the time children enter a formal classroom they have a considerable knowledge about letters and sounds. Once, on a long car trip at night, two-year-old Kristin's dad stopped for ice cream. Not wanting to wake Kristin, he whispered the letters I-C-E-C-R-E-A-M to ask Averil if she wanted some, too. Within a few seconds, the previously sleeping Kristin piped up from the car seat and said, "I want I-D-P too!" Although she could not have known what the letters spelled, she most certainly knew that they represented something good to eat. More than twenty years later, ice cream is still called I-D-P by Kristin's family. This information about letters and sounds can be used to develop their ability to read, write, and spell in the early years of schooling.

Learning: A Developmental Process

Figure 1.1 outlines some of the characteristics that take place during your child's speech and language development. In the chapters that follow we want to show that learning to read, write, and spell is also a developmental process. You used your observational skills to know when to prevent your children from falling once they started to walk, and you spent countless hours reading stories, talking, and singing to your children. When you were not sure of some part of her development you may have consulted a book. Your parents probably kept a copy of Dr. Spock's *Baby and Childcare* handy. Parents in the seventies and eighties viewed this book as an expert source. (Some still refer to it.) Today, many parents keep medical books in the house to check on some aspect of development or to find out more when their children are ill. As teachers, our formal schooling taught us about the developmental nature of literacy. As parents as well as teachers, one of our goals is to provide you with a text that you can refer to whenever you are confronted with an issue regarding your child's literacy.

More important, research offers figures on the amount of time children spend at home versus the amount of time they spend at school. For example, in the United Kingdom, from the time a child is born until sixteen years of age, she or he spends 15 percent of her or his time in school (MacBeth). For the United States and Canada, those percentages are 9 (Murphy) and 13 (Oglan) respectively. Therefore, we offer you strategies and ideas that can be used to help enhance development at home.

According to these figures, children in North America spend an average of 87–91 percent of their time from birth to age sixteen outside school. Of course, the time spent outside school must take into account other things such as household chores, music lessons, sports teams, church activities, and so on. Also, there are interests such as computers, video games, and cable television that compete with school. By providing parents with information on the developmental nature of learning to read, write, and spell, we feel parents will be in a better position to know when and what to look for and how to support their children when they are not at school.

The nice part is that many of the strategies we describe are not like the traditional work you had when you were in school. Your involvement at times will be informal and casual. It may even take place outside the home while traveling to a piano lesson or driving someone to a hockey practice. Other times, it may require that you invest more

Birth to Eight Months	Eight to Eighteen Months	Toddlers and Two-Year-Olds (Eighteen Months–Three Years)
• Cries to signal pain. • Smiles or vocalizes to initiate social contact. • Responds to human voices. Gazes at faces. • Uses vocal and nonvocal communication to express interest and exert influece. • Babbles using all types of sounds. Engages in private conversation when alone. • Combines babbles. Understands names of familiar people and objects. Laughs. Listens to conversations.	• Understands many more words than can say. Looks toward 20 or more objects when named. • Creates long, babbled sentences. • Shakes head no. Says two or three clear words. • Looks at picture books with interest, points to objects. • Uses vocal signals other than crying to gain assistance. • Begins to use *me, you, I*.	• Combines words. • Listens to stories for a short while. • Develops fantasy in language. Begins to play pretend games. • Defines use of many household items. • Uses compound sentences. • Uses adjectives and adverbs. Recounts events of the day.

Figure 1.1. Developmental milestones for communication (Bredekamp & Copple, 1997).

time at home working with your child. Your role will change from the person who answers questions to someone who learns how to ask questions.

We would like to offer one caution. Although a number of parents and teachers successfully used many of the strategies presented here, we can offer no guarantees. Will they work every time? all of the time? with all children? Of course not. We do not expect everything to work all of the time with every child. Our intent is to provide you with strategies and suggestions to use and with resources to help you to work more effectively with your children. If you encounter difficulties, another parent or friend with whom you can discuss your situation often helps. Talk to your child's teachers to let them know what you are doing. Many schools now have parent groups that meet regularly, supporting parents as they work with their children at home.

Parent Story: Manon Lacroix, H. D. Taylor Public School, Windsor, Ontario

My daughter who just turned five was trying to tell my three-year-old daughter a story. As I watched them, I realized the value of letting children pretend to tell and read stories and not to interrupt. I also found that reading and talking about street signs/billboards, and so on, helps children to learn the alphabet. My three-year-old gets lots of practice with sounds and letters on our trips just by looking at highway signs. As she reads the signs we talk about the words and letters on the signs. Sometimes, we play the alphabet game where we try to find signs that begin with the letters of the alphabet. My eight-year-old learns geography, and she can tell me the cities between Windsor and Toronto. As we get close to a city, she reads the signs and we talk about the cities. Even though I have heard the same story often, I now know it is important for her to talk about it while I listen and try to offer a little more information. She knows that Chatham is one-fourth of the way and that London is one-half of the way. As a result of speaking and listening to my children, I feel I am able to understand fragments of words in my eight-year-old daughter's written work. I can now see where speaking and listening help my children when they read and write.

Strategies for Listening and Speaking to Use at Home

- Ask your child to tell you about her day at school. Don't accept a response such as "fine" or "nothing happened today." If you must begin the conversation, start by asking questions about specific subjects or about certain friends or upcoming events at the school.
- When reading a story or watching a television program, ask children to predict what they think might happen next. Predicting activates thinking. Once the predictions are made, discuss differences or similarities between what actually happened and their predictions. This is a way to confirm the accuracy of information. We usually find that boys are more reluctant to offer information than girls are. However, interest is a key component and this is where parents can get involved. Start with sports. Hockey, baseball, and basketball playoffs are a great time to make predictions and follow-up.
- Whenever the family gathers, try this listening game. One person starts by whispering a word in the first person's ear (for example, "farmer"). The person has to then whisper the word to the next person and add a word ("old farmer"). By the time it gets to the last person they have to say all of the words out loud so everyone can hear ("Old farmer fed the cows"). For young children you might begin with one word; for older children, however, you might try starting with a short sentence. This game is fun and generates a lot of discussion about who said what.
- When your children ask you if they can go to a friend's, tell them they have to come up with a convincing argument highlighting all of the reasons (good and bad) why you should say "yes."
- If you are traveling in a car with older kids or you are in a grocery store with younger children, ask them to give you directions on how to get to and from certain places.
- Pretend to be a robot and ask your children to give you directions on how to make a peanut butter sandwich.
- If you have a video camera or cassette recorder, encourage your children to make their own skits and plays or radio broadcasts. Remember that it is equally important that you watch or listen to these productions.

- Ask your children to select an object from inside the cupboard and describe as many features and uses for the object as they can.
- Read to your children on a regular basis. Pause frequently and discuss parts of the story. Ask questions such as, "What would you have done if you were the king?" or "If you were the author of this book, what would you have done differently?" (More reading strategies will be discussed in Chapter 2.)

Reflections

These strategies are not only meant to act as a starting point for working with your children, they are also for your own learning. Whenever you are together with other parents, share some of these strategies and invite other parents to share what they do with their children to help promote speaking and listening at home. Your child's classroom teacher is another good resource for listening and speaking strategies. We began this chapter with questions parents ask about speaking and listening. The research on the relationship between speaking and listening and reading and writing indicates that these components of language should develop simultaneously. Predicting before reading or talking about a topic before writing allows speaking and listening to enhance reading and writing. In Chapter 2, we look at the developmental nature of learning to read, and in Chapter 3 we will look at writing and spelling. If you have questions of your own based on this chapter, take a few moments to write them down and then share them with other parents or teachers in hopes of finding answers.

> "The relationship between speech and action is a dynamic one. Children not only speak about what they are doing; their speech and actions are part of one and the same psychological function, directed toward solving the problem at hand."
> Vygotsky, 1986

Lingering Thoughts

Based on my reading of this chapter I am wondering about the following:

_____

_____

_____

_____

_____

_____

_____

_____

_____

2 Readers and Reading

- How do I get my son to understand what he has read?
- When is it okay to correct a child when she is reading?
- If I read out loud to my kids, should I have them read to me?
- What is the best way to teach a child to read?
- How do you deal with a child who can read but does not want to try?

Children discover and uncover how language works by using it on a regular basis. Your children learned to talk because you spoke to them, and with them. In doing so, you taught them about speech by modeling and demonstrating spoken language. Learning to read (and write and spell) are the same things. The single most important factor influencing children's literacy is the amount of time someone reads to them (Bialostok, 1992). The parent who "lap-reads" to a baby helps that child associate books and reading with love. Averil occasionally has children who come to school in kindergarten already knowing how to read. The parents of these children often claim that they did not teach them to read. At one time, these children were labeled as gifted, and people thought that they were just born to read. Research, however, indicates that children who are "born readers" come from homes in which people read to themselves and to others—in which children were surrounded by print: magazines, newspapers, and books.

Most parents agree that reading to their children is important. Why? Because when you read to a child, the child has an opportunity to hear the flow and rhythm of the language. Don't be afraid to read books to your children that may seem beyond their own reading ability. They are able to understand at a higher level when you read to them than when they read alone. Research indicates that children who were read to from birth have an advantage over children who come from homes where reading is not valued. Many researchers agree that reading to children for fifteen minutes a day would revolutionize schools.

Paul Kropp (1993), a researcher who has studied parents and their impact on reading to children, identified two critical times in children's lives when they "turn off" reading. The first is what he calls the "grade-four factor." He says that when children reach grade four, many parents feel that they are old enough to read on their own and simply stop reading to them. According to Kropp, this is a wrong assumption for parents to make. Children at this grade and age level benefit from being read to because it keeps them interested, provides them with an ongoing model of how competent readers approach a text, helps them concentrate on the story and not the words, as well as learn about intonation and how grammar works. Reading to your children demonstrates to them that you value reading and the time you spend with them. When time is so precious to everyone, the message you send is "I love you and to prove it I am willing to read with you."

Kropp believes that you should continue to read to your children into their high school years. The second critical time in a child's life is what he calls the "grade-nine factor." Some parents equate grade nine with independence. Children starting high school are expected to "grow up" and be responsible enough to read on their own. However, learning patterns in children entering grade nine show that initially their marks decline. Why? Some of this is due to the transition from the physical size of their elementary schools to the much larger high school settings. Many students are just not prepared to handle the freedom and responsibility of high school. Students are also dealing with puberty, relationships, pimples, and "fitting in." When older kids limit their reading to only homework activities, reading is reduced to something that "has to be done" and never something to enjoy.

Reading with your older children demonstrates two important points. First, it's a way for you to stay up-to-date on their work at school. When children know that you will be expecting information from them, they take more responsibility for their actions. Second, whether they say it or not they enjoy the contact with you through the interest that you show. Also, reading together emphasizes the value of reading. You might even read the novel they have been assigned in school and then have a conversation about likes and dislikes. This one strategy can pay off because it demonstrates to your child that your actions speak louder than words. At the same time, you model and demonstrate through your actions that you care (just as you did when they were learning to talk).

Reading with your children helps them gain self-confidence in their own reading. As your child's self-confidence increases, you may notice that her interests and focus may broaden to different kinds of reading, such as catalogs, signs, manuals, menus, TV guides, and the like (Goodman & Marek, 1996).

Figure 2.1 is a sign that Averil's (then) eight-year-old daughter, Greer, made for her bedroom door. One evening while Greer and Averil were trying to enjoy some time together, it seemed as if other members of the family kept interrupting them. In desperation to claim this time with her mom, Greer made the sign and hung it on the door. Greer

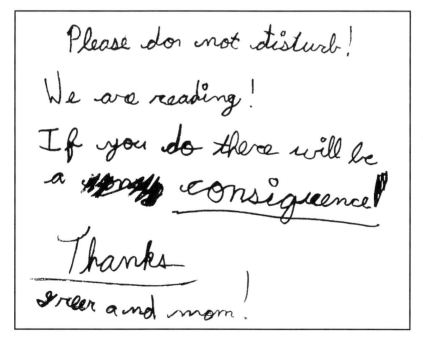

Figure 2.1. Greer's sign to the rest of the family.

knew that her written message would be more powerful than a spoken one. Perhaps you can relate to this story if you have young children who enjoy creating signs and hanging them around the house for everyone to read. Bedroom doors seem to be the most popular places. Children and teenagers view bedrooms as "private property," and they like to let everyone who enters the house know that this area is "their space."

Predicting, Sampling, and Confirming

In Chapter 1 we mentioned that reading, like viewing and listening, involves predicting, sampling, and confirming text. Before a child listens to a story or reads a story on her own, it is important to encourage her to make predictions about the story. Why? Predicting activates whatever prior knowledge a person has about a particular topic or subject and brings it to a conscious level of awareness. To help you understand how this might be done, let's look at reading the story *Grandma's Secret*.

To start, read the title and ask your child what she thinks the story might be about, discuss any key words that may lead to a prediction, and examine the cover pictures and discuss clues that point toward the meaning of the story. During predicting ask *why?* This question pushes the reader's thinking because she has to explain predictions, providing you with a source to her thinking and activating whatever information she has about the story or similar stories. Offer a prediction of your own, too!

With this information activated, sample the text by starting to read. Pause throughout the text when you think your child can confirm or reject a prediction based on what was read. Have a discussion and ask questions. Asking questions is a key in the development of understanding and reading comprehension (for more questioning strategies, see the section on reading comprehension).

- What do you think will happen next? Why?
- If you were _____ what would you have done?
- How do you know that?
- Where in the story does it say that?
- What do you think they should do?
- What new predictions can you now make? Why?

Through questioning, the child must explain why she responded as she did. Explaining is important because it reinforces the child's ability to recall information and make it explicit. It supports a connection between thought and language (Vygotsky, 1986). If her predictions are off the mark, avoid saying, "that's wrong." In fact, it's best to avoid any negative statements. You want your child to develop a sense of confidence by knowing the answers she gives are valued. Predicting, sampling, and confirming can be used when you read a story or can be taught as a strategy to use when the child reads on her own. This strategy is also helpful for teenagers to use when they have to summarize the main points of a story. Once predictions are confirmed they become the main points to the story. Students can take the confirmed predictions and write a book report or a summary. Teach them to make predictions before they read, and when they start to read, stop periodically to think about their predictions and make new predictions. Strategies that support predicting, sampling, and confirming can be found at the end of this chapter.

Reading Comprehension

When you think about reading comprehension, you might have memories of your school days. The teacher assigned a story that you read silently, and then you were assigned a series of questions based on the story. The number of questions you answered correctly determined how well the teacher thought you read or comprehended the story. Reading research now supports a different approach to comprehension based on "meaning" and the "prior knowledge" of the reader. Prior knowledge is defined as experiences children bring to the text and the amount of exposure they have to a variety of topics. A child whose family spends time camping will bring those life experiences to a story that takes place in a national park. A child who lives in the city with an elderly grandparent and travels very little will not have the same knowledge of campfires and rattlesnakes.

Comprehension takes into account three systems of language referred to as the semantic system (prior knowledge), syntactic system (grammar, word order), and the graphophonemic system (letter-sound relationships). These three systems work together to help a reader construct the meaning of a text. To demonstrate how this works, read the story, "The Cordanic," and then answer the comprehension questions that follow (story and questions from Weaver, 1994).

> The Cordanic is an emurient grof with many fribs; it granks from corite, an olg which cargs like lange. Corite grinkles several other tarances, which garkers excarp by glarcking the corite and starping it in tranker-clarped storbs. The tarances starp a chark which is exasperated with worters, branking a slorp. This slorp is garped through several corusces, finally frasting a pragety, blickant crankle: coranda. Coranda is a cargurt, grinkling corandic and borigen. The corandic is narcerated from the borigen by means of loracity. Thus garkers finally thrap a glick, bracht, glupous, grapant, cordanic, which granks in many sarps.
>
> 1. What is a cordanic?
> 2. What does it grank from?
> 3. How do garkers excarp the trances from the corite?

As you read this story, all three systems were at work. First you used your knowledge about letters and sounds (graphophonemics) to identify and sound out the words. Your syntactic system helped you identify possible verbs, nouns, adjective, adverbs, articles, and so on. The text has all the characteristics of the English language, and if I were to ask you to read it out loud you would have probably stumbled over a few words, but you would have gotten through it. The one system that you struggled with was the semantic (prior knowledge) system. Even though you could read the text and the words, you had no prior knowledge about the Cordanic or any of the characters to draw on. Therefore, all meaning was lost. What about the comprehension questions, though? Did you get all three answers correct?

> 1. emurient grof
> 2. from corite
> 3. By glarcking the corite and starping it in tranker-clarped storbs.

Many parents are able to answer all three questions. If this were a comprehension test, they would have successfully answered three out of three questions correctly, resulting in a score of 100 percent or an A +. However, if I were to ask them to draw a Cordanic or a scene from the story, it would be impossible because the semantic system was not functioning.

Comprehension, Retellings, and Miscues

W hen working with your children, remember that all three systems (semantics, syntax, graphophonemics) work together. This may mean that as children read they may leave out words, or insert words to help them establish the meaning of the text. Good readers do this all the time. If you want to help develop reading comprehension, begin by asking them to make predictions based on what they think the story is about. If they can read, let them read the story silently, or you read the story to them and then ask them to retell the story to you.

Reading silently allows them to make miscues. Miscues are words or parts of the text that readers consciously or unconsciously leave out or insert in the interest of establishing meaning. If they do read out loud, do not attempt to correct them. If anything, encourage them to guess at a word and then read on (see Oral Reading). When they have finished they should retell the story, or talk about what they read. Start by asking the following questions (Rhodes & Shanklin, 1993):

Questions for Narratives (Stories with a Plot and Characters)

Character Recall:	Who was in the story?
	Who else was in the story?
Character Development:	What else can you tell me about _____?
Setting:	Where did _____ happen?
	When did _____ happen?
	Tell me more about _____ place?
Events:	What else happened in the story?
	How did _____ happen?
Event Sequence:	What happened before _____ ?
	What happened after _____ ?
Plot:	What was _____ main problem?
Theme:	What did you think (major character) learned from the story?
	What do you think the author might have been trying to tell us in this story?

Questions to Use with an Expository Text (Informational Text)

Major Concept(s):   What was the main thing the author wanted
                       you to learn?

Generalizations: What other important information about _____
                       did the author tell you?

Specific Information: Is there any other information you remember
                       the author told about?
                       What specific facts do you remember?

Logical Structuring: How did the author go about presenting the
                       information? (comparison, examples, steps in
                       the process, etc.)

Questions serve as a guide for your children to tell everything they read about the story. Children who cannot retell stories may be reading word by word and not establishing meaning. Some children can read an entire story perfectly, without understanding the story. Strategies such as Say Something, Read Alouds, Sketch to Stretch, and Think Alouds (found in the strategy section) will help your child to read for meaning.

Oral Reading

When parents listen to their children read they become concerned about hesitations, insertions, or mispronunciation of words. It is important that parents not interfere and provide the word for the child. This is very hard for parents who were brought up in a system that corrected children the minute they could not pronounce a word. Maybe you can remember those days during your schooling when everyone in the class was asked to read out loud. Remember sitting and waiting for the teacher to call your name? Remember how nervous you were? Good readers often omit many words because they are able to predict the meaning of the words based on the text that comes before the words and the text that comes after the words. This can be demonstrated by reading the following text

Bear Cubs

New bear cubs are so _____. They can't see well. They can't get things to _____. But they are cute! When cubs are so little they do not go _____. The mother bear gives her cubs all that they need. Soon the _____ are not so little. They go out with their _____.

Everything is new to the cubs! They want to see _____. The cubs have a good time jumping, rolling, and ____.

In order to read this passage you had to rely on the information that came before and after the blanks to predict what words would best fit the meaning of the sentences and also fit with the entire meaning of the story. This is what good readers do. They use the information before and after to make accurate predictions.

When your children read with you (use the bear cub story), teach them to use the clues in the story to help them make predictions about the words they are trying to pronounce (see the section at the end of this chapter on Cloze Passages). When children do this they have a self-editing device that tells them when they have said a word that fits the meaning of the sentence. The following sentence from the bear cub story can be used to demonstrate this. In the last sentence of the story one child read, "The cubs have a good time jumping rolling, and sleeping." The word "sleeping" did not really fit with jumping and rolling. When we asked him why he used the word "sleeping," he said that he knew that new babies sleep and thought it would be the same for the cubs. Although he used his prior knowledge about sleeping babies, he did not use the text that came before (and after, had there been another sentence) to confirm or reject whether his prediction fit the meaning of the story. If he had done so, his internal meaning editor would have told him that "sleeping" does not fit with jumping and rolling. When we read the sentence back to him he self-corrected and said that "sleeping" did not fit and substituted the word "playing," which fit the meaning of the sentence and the story.

When some children read orally, they spend most of their time sounding out rather than using the clues from the text to gain meaning. Did you know that you leave out text when you read silently? If we could monitor your brain when you read silently, we would find that you mispronounce words, leave out words, and put in words that don't belong. *But you still get the meaning.* You would also find that you do a lot of self-correcting in the process so that you can follow the plot. How often have you gone back to reread something in a book or paper because it didn't make sense? Your children are no different when they read. One of the reasons your children may be reluctant to read out loud is because they think that a good reader can pronounce or read every word. While listening to your children read, if they come to a word they do not know, ask them to

- Look at the illustrations for clues
- Think about the title and what the story is about
- Choose a word that they think might fit
- Reread the sentence and ask themselves if the word they chose fits the meaning of the sentence and the story
- Keep reading if they are satisfied with their word choice

Your children should not rely only on "sounding out" as their primary strategy. Teach them to look before and after the word and use this information to make a prediction. Once the child has finished reading the entire text or story, come back to the words that she either mispronounced or substituted and tell her what she said and what the text said. At this point ask her why she made a certain substitution or pronunciation. Through this discussion you will be developing your child's ability to read orally and comprehend better by using these strategies.

Some developing readers rely only on sounding out as a strategy. As a result, their ability to comprehend decreases because they use all of their time and energy relying on sound. If children approach reading as making meaning, and if they can use multiple strategies, your level of frustration will decrease and your children's level of confidence will increase. They will view themselves as more capable readers. To further help you assist your children with this goal, we have included a list of books for Kindergarten through grade 8 (see Appendix A) from which you can choose books to read with your children. During workshops, parents were always eager for strategies to use at home. Most of the strategies that follow can be used with children at any age or grade level, although some may require a few modifications.

Parent Story: Sue Silver, Windsor, Ontario

It's a funny thing when someone asks you to remember some of the literacy things you've done with your children (now ages twelve and eight). It's difficult to remember all the things I've done. I guess I remember the ones that were the most fun for me. I loved the writing in the sand and snow with a stick or with stones. Of course, there were visits to the library and stores to borrow and purchase books. I liked it when they started to read signs and billboards and the challenge of seeing what they were talking about before we drove by it. My daughter went through a whole winter of writing on the sweaty windows in the car. She would make up new words and sound them out. She seemed to understand the phonetic concept—something that I still struggle with because my literacy strategies are memory based. Unfortunately, my son is also a memory-based reader and has a lot of difficulty with phonics, especially with vowel sounds. He is in the third grade and has a new teacher who believes in teacher-directed spelling lists with a test every Friday. We practice on Wednesdays and Thursdays so that he will experience success and not hate writing totally. He is successful on Fridays but by Saturday has forgotten the words; for example, I asked him to add the word "windows" to my to-do list on Saturday, and he said he didn't know how to spell it. I reminded him he could spell the first part of the word "win" because it was on his Friday list. "Oh Mom, that was just for my test." He definitely didn't transfer his information from short-term to long-term memory! We are great list makers—jobs-to-do lists, grocery lists, wish lists, vacation lists, and so on. We all add to each other's lists. We write to relatives via mail or e-mail. The computer has definitely extended literacy. My son loves to type in any word into a program that will read it back to you. It's a challenge to see if the computer knows all the words he knows. My daughter continues to be an avid writer—it's often the way she spends her free time. My son is not interested and needs encouragement (or a reason) to read or write (sports magazines, comics, birthday wish lists, etc.). I guess out of all the literacy activities, I enjoy the bed-time story the most. There is nothing like reading or hearing a story with your children when everyone is snuggled up. The warmth, the smell, the sounds—all add up to wonderful feelings (and memories) around reading. I almost forgot one of the most important things to do in order to encourage your children's literacy, and it's one of the easiest for me to do. I instill a love of reading because I simply love to read.

Strategies for Reading to Use at Home

Read Alouds

This is a common strategy used by parents. Read Alouds take place when an adult reads to a child. The purpose is for enjoyment and provides both the parent and the child an opportunity to spend some quality time together. Children may either ask questions or offer comments. Read Alouds give the opportunity to hear experienced readers reading stories. We call this lap reading—when we read to babies and toddlers.

Think Alouds

Think Alouds help to activate prior knowledge. As the title implies, a Think Aloud begins by talking out loud about the subject or topic, saying anything that comes to mind. It works best when done with a partner because it allows for an exchange of ideas and information to take place.

Sketching and Drawing

Young children like to draw or sketch. After reading a story, invite them to draw their favorite part. After they complete their sketches, ask them to tell you why they drew a particular picture. Use this as an opportunity to talk about other details of the story.

Say Something

Say Something is a strategy that will help your child develop his ability to comprehend a story. It does help if you have two copies of the story to be read but it can also be accomplished using a single copy. To begin, you read a paragraph or section of the text silently and then say something to your child about what you just read. Allow your child to read the next paragraph or part of the text and invite him to comment on what he just read. As each of you reads silently and shares what you read, you will probably begin to discuss certain sections of the story that may relate to the characters, plot, setting, and so on. Continue taking turns reading and sharing until you finish the story.

Retellings

If children have a story to read from school or if you want them to read one from their collection at home, a Retelling is a nice way to see if they have an understanding of what they read. This is often referred to as reading comprehension. It is important to ask questions and not provide them with your interpretations of the story. The best way to begin is to ask, "So tell me everything you know about this story." Allow the child to recall as much as she can. Encourage her to take her time and tell you as much as she can. When you think she has exhausted her memory, ask her questions (see the section on reading comprehension, narrative and expository retellings).

Audiotape

Children like to play with tape recorders. Let them read a story on to a tape and then listen to it. You might even record some of their favorite stories on tape for situations when you are not available to read with them. Also, record stories that they would like to read, although they might feel somewhat intimidated by the text. These stories make good traveling activities in the car or van. You might want to keep an audiotape of their reading throughout the year and save them from year to year.

Book Talks: Reading with Older Children

If you have children in grades six and up who are reluctant readers or who may be losing interest in reading, you might try reading some of their novels and books from school. By doing this, you can have a Book Talk. Book Talks can take place over the dinner table, in the car, or in the evenings. Start a Book Talk by asking a question related to the story such as, "What did you think of what happened in chapter one?" If your children respond in short answers, keep asking them for more information by asking other questions, such as, "What do you mean by that?" or "Tell me more about _____." Find books around their interest (hockey, werewolves, movie stars, etc.).

Cloze Passages

If you want to help your children read for meaning and improve their comprehension, Cloze Passages are very useful. Take a story from the reader, or use a story from home (such as "The Bear Cub"). It should

be a story that your children have not read before. The age and grade
level of your children will determine the length of the story you select.
Photocopy the story and then select words to delete. Most texts have
two types of words: content words and function words. Content words
carry most of the meaning, while function words are usually preposi-
tions, articles, and sight words. Using liquid paper, delete at least one
content word from each sentence. Next, photocopy the passage to use
with your child. Have your children read the text, and when they come
to the blank, encourage them to read the text before and after the
blank, as well as think about the meaning of the entire story. Whatever
answer they give, leave it and move on until they have completed the
entire story. Then go back through the text, discussing the words they
used and why.

Homemade Storybooks

Young children love stories, and they love to make things. Take
advantage of this interest by writing down your child's story as he tells it
to you in his own words. Arrange the pages in order and make it into a
book. Remember that he is the author and should make all decisions
regarding the content and design; allow him to choose the cover and
paper. Read it back to him so that he can hear it, and have him "read" it
back to you. This exercise conveys the message that there is meaning in
print and that print is "talk" written down. You can even make copies of
these books and let your child give them as gifts.

Cooking

Cooking and books are a great combination for home. Your child
can help you make pancakes after you read *Pancakes* by Eric Carle, or
want to eat porridge after a Retelling of *The Three Bears*. Older children
can help you by reading the ingredients from recipes as you cook
together. Children of all ages like to help make up their own recipes for
things. You could start a family cookbook.

Cereal Box Books

By cutting out the front of empty boxes of your family's favorite
cereal, punching a hole in them and running a string or ring through
the holes, your child will have a book that she can read over and over
again. At first, she may only read the pictures; later, though, she will
also begin to see the similarities in words and letters. The same can be

done with grocery bags from every place you shop. Fold them into their original shapes and staple together along one edge to make a book. Soon your child will read Kroger, Wal-Mart, K-Mart, Gap, and so on.

Labels

Children in kindergarten and early primary classrooms label things that are important to them—such as Books, Bathroom, Computer, and so on. You can have your child do the same at home. Let her print the word on a card and label the object. Talk about the important words and other words that sound or look similar. Add labels gradually, as your child suggests them.

Electronic Mail

If you have a computer, encourage your children to send messages and letters to friends and relatives. This could be done cooperatively with young children. They can dictate and you can type it, as they watch their words turn into print.

Reflections

In this chapter we attempted to demonstrate that reading is more than identifying words. Learners of all ages develop reading competency through the contact and verbal exchanges they experience with other learners. Much of your child's success depends on the time you set aside to work with them.

> **"Individuals become literate, not from the formal instruction they receive, but what they read, and who they read it with."**
> **Smith, 1992**

Sometimes it is easier not to get involved with our children or their literacy development and leave it in the hands of the schools. Each family is different, and times spent together will vary. The key to academic success is an awareness and involvement on your part to be actively involved in your child's literacy development. You may want to take a few moments and write down any questions or concerns you have about this chapter. Take them and share them with other parents and educators to help you resolve some of the issues you feel will help you to help your children.

Lingering Thoughts

_____

_____

_____

_____

_____

_____

_____

_____

_____

3 Writing and Spelling

- When should a parent insist on correct spelling?
- Is sounding out the best way for all children to learn to spell?
- Do you correct the wrong spelling right away?
- What makes a child interested in reading, yet not at all interested in writing?

In this chapter we will look at writing and spelling development in a variety of "texts," for example, shopping lists, letters, editorials, thank-you notes, postcards, and various forms of creative writing. We will also address the concerns expressed by parents regarding writing and speaking "correct" English. Since we know that young children do not always use "correct" grammar when they are learning to talk, we as parents must adopt a similar trust when they begin to write.

Beginning Writers

As children are learning to write, they naturally make many errors as they practice and experiment. At first, they will write no real words, and later they progress to a point where they recognize a few words, usually found in environmental print. Developmentally, they go from having more words wrong than right to more words right than wrong. If we stress accuracy all of the time, they may shy away from experimenting with new words and enlarging their vocabulary. Eventually they lose sight of the real purpose of writing—to communicate. It is important to resist the temptation to criticize. Instead, emphasize your child's successes. We need to look for the ways in which our children are smart and not focus on their errors. We need to support our child's first attempts at writing by providing materials and opportunities and celebrating growth as it occurs. As you support your child's attempts at writing, encourage friends and family members to give gifts that support writing as well. These might include books, calligraphy pens, pads of paper, computer paper, nontoxic correction fluid, dictionaries, thesauri, blank books, and journals or diaries.

When young children start to write, they use nonstandard text. Nonstandard text is often referred to as "scribble writing," as seen in Figure 3.1. They do this for a couple of reasons. By watching adults, they know that writing is used to communicate messages, and they imitate their parents or other adults by using this form of writing. It is important for us to recognize scribble writing as *writing* and not just scribbling. If your child produces a piece of writing in nonstandard form ask him to read his "story" to you. Yes, refer to it as a story. This is important because it says to your children that you value what they

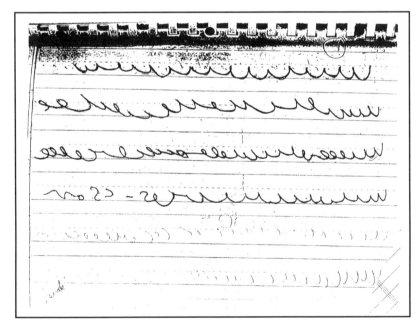

Figure 3.1. An example of scribble writing.

write. Acknowledging it as a story places it on the same level as your writing.

The more children hear stories read, and see print around them, the more they learn about written language. When children realize that the letters of the alphabet are used to represent and communicate messages, they begin to incorporate what they are learning into their mature writing—sometimes referred to as representational writing (see Figure 3.2).

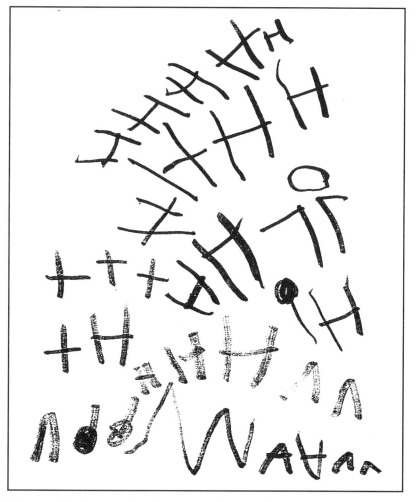

Figure 3.2. An example of representational writing.

When teachers ask children to write or print their own names, some children report that they cannot write. We encourage them to write what they know. When their efforts are acknowledged, they begin to feel like writers and thereby develop the confidence to take more risks and experiment with their writing.

In representational writing children use strings of letters to make up their stories. At times you can detect the beginning of words that are represented by a single letter. This also marks the beginning of spelling, since, in order to write, the child is relying on what they know about letters and sounds and their relationship to each other.

Figure 3.3. Jarrod's dinosaur story.

Soon you may begin to see spaces that mark the beginning and ending of words. When looking at your child's writing, look for what they know about language words (see Figure 3.3). In Jarrod's story we see the following:

- It is organized from left to right, top to bottom.
- A drawing supports his message.
- Spaces separate words.
- An attempt is made to spell "tyrannosaurus."

At this point children begin to write stories that are usually accompanied by a picture or drawing. They do this because they know that pictures carry meaning. Figure 3.4 is a story that Alexis, a grade 1

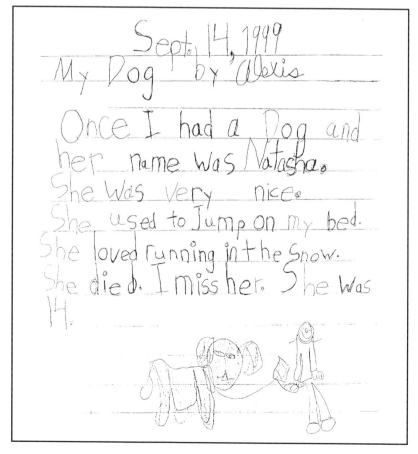

Figure 3.4. Alexis's story about her dog.

student, wrote. In her story, we can see she is using spacing, illustration, capitals, and punctuation. Knowing what to look for can help you determine how your child is developing. Try not to focus on errors; rather, stress what they do know. In studying the spelling patterns of young children, Gerry identified spelling strategies that may be helpful to you when you look at your child's writing (see Figure 3.5).

---

1. Letter Name
   Each letter of a word says the name of the letter. Vowels are usually absent, e.g., first/frst, letter/ltr.
2. Spelling as it sounds
   Students rely on the sounds they hear that are close to the actual sound, for example, uncle/uncul, feather/fethir.
3. Placeholder
   When spelling words with vowels, students will replace one vowel with another that is similar in sound, for example, went/wont, video/vedio.
4. Representations
   Students sometimes know that a vowel is needed but insert a random vowel, for example, misery/maziry, sometime/semtim.
5. Overgeneralizations
   When students discover a new structure such as the silent e at the end of words, they see it exclusively, for example, won/wone, from/frome
6. Transpositional
   Words that are spelled using all of the correct letters but are in the wrong order, for example, tried/tride, watch/wacht.
7. Visual
   Words have a visual likeness to the conventional form, for example, school/scool, teacher/techer.
8. Articulation
   Vowels and consonants are close in sound and are usually used interchangeably, for example, combat/kombat graphics/grafics.
9. One letter misses
   The word is close to the conventional form with the exception of a letter, for example, snowed/snowd, waiting/wating.
10. Multiple Strategies
    This involves combinations of the strategies, for example, neighborhood/nebrhode, retirement/ritearment.

Figure 3.5. Spelling strategies identified by Oglan (1997).

Remember, these strategies are meant to act as a guide; they are not exclusive and you may see variations. Many people have referred to the incorrect spellings that children produce as "invented spelling" or "sloppy spelling." We prefer the term "functional spellings" because they serve a function when the child is writing. The function is to "place-hold" the meaning of a word by using a spelling that is either close to the actual word or that represents the correct form. They are not wrong if what the child is trying to communicate succeeds.

Let's look at another piece of writing that Jarrod wrote when he was in grade 2. At the end of a long day, Jarrod acted out in class and was caught by the teacher, who told him to write a note to his mother explaining what he had done (see Figure 3.6). Look at what Jarrod knows about spelling, grammar, and punctuation (use the strategies as a guide). In this piece, we can see that he knows how a letter is written by the opening, "Mom," and the closing, "Love Jarrod." He uses contractions (I've) and capitalizes the first person pronoun (I). He used sounding-out strategies (no. 2) for "brot/brought," "rot/wrote," "feger/finger," and "not/note." When he spelled "signed/singed" on his first attempt, he used a transpositional spelling (no. 6), and when he wrote "sign" on his second attempt, he spelled it correctly. When children spell words with all of the correct letters present but in the wrong order, we suggest you

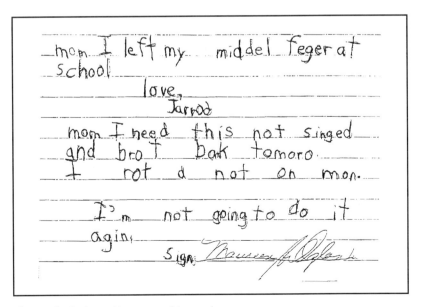

Figure 3.6. Jarrod's note to his mother.

not worry about these types of spellings because they tell us that the child is about to internalize the correct spelling. On the word tomoro/ tomorrow, he knew how to spell the word "to." He added "moro," but if he had included the letter "w," his spelling would have been only one letter away from being correct.

When children spell words with double consonants the only way for them to know the correct spelling is to internalize it. This comes with seeing it many times, which is why we emphasize the importance of reading to and with your child. On the word left/lift he used a place-hold strategy (no. 3) because the short "e" is close in sound to the short "i." When parents ask me about the spelling of the word "agin," I suspect that some of the southern dialect was influencing his spelling. We were in South Carolina at the time.

Rethinking Error

We were brought up to look for error. Consequently, when you look at a piece of writing your child has produced, you automatically see what is wrong, as opposed to what your child knows about language. Look from a different point-of-view and try doing a "word count." In Jarrod's story, I counted all of the words and found that he used a total of thirty-four words to write his note. Of these, twelve were functional spellings, which left twenty-four as correct spellings. Jarrod spelled 70 percent of his words accurately. Remember that transpositional spelling and one-letter misses are spellings your child is in the process of internalizing correctly. If we eliminate these, his accuracy rate increases to 75 percent. His functional spellings can be explained based on what he knows about sounds, letters, and their relationship to each other, and about how language works. We can use this knowledge to help Jarrod see the differences between the words he spelled and the correct forms of the words. We do this by simply writing them with him and discussing the patterns so that he will have this information for future use.

Figure 3.7 shows a postcard that Greer (age 7) wrote from camp to her grandmother. She begins with, "Dear Mary" because her mother had already addressed the card that way. Notice what Greer understands about letter writing and spelling. She uses a salutation, closing, and signature. Excluding the word "Mary," which she copied, thirty-seven words are spelled correctly. All of the words are spelled using a sounding out strategy. At the age of seven, Greer knows a lot about phonics and spelling. Also, she uses punctuation correctly as well as capitals at the beginning of every sentence. Learning about phonics is enhanced when children themselves are experimenting with writing, since they will be thinking about sounds and symbols as they write.

Working with Older Children

When Averil taught grade 5, she encouraged children to write regularly and, although many of the students could think of topics on their own, Averil always chose a topic for the class, mistakenly thinking this would help the more "reluctant" writers in her room. Nathan, a student in her class, taught her that this strategy had the opposite effect. Although he was a very bright student, his stories always seemed to come up short. Before long, writing seemed to become painful for Nathan. A budding hockey player, Nathan was also struggling with fine motor skills necessary for handwriting. He was

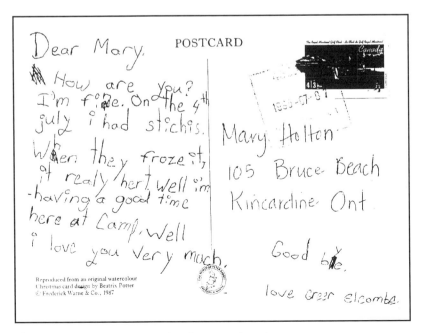

Figure 3.7. Greer's postcard to her grandmother.

becoming more and more frustrated by the daily chore of writing about what his teacher thought was interesting. Every day, Nathan struggled to satisfy his teacher's expectations, until the day they sat together for a writing conference. Averil asked him why he did not like to write anymore and his answer surprised her. He told her that he really wanted to write a novel about hockey—he just did not like to write at school!

After that day, Nathan always chose what he wanted to write. He began to write his novel on the computer and continues to be an avid writer today. This story has interesting ramifications for us as parents. If we want our children to be writers, we have to let them write. Averil loves to write about her children and her life experiences, but not about fly fishing or the rainforests, both very interesting subjects to many people. If we want children to write, we need to let them write about what is interesting to them—not about what is interesting to us.

Writing and Story Length

One pattern we like to point out to parents has to do with the length of a written story. Many students are led to believe that the length of a story is a sign of a good writer. Gerry's son, Jarrod, was working on an essay for his ninth-grade English class when Gerry noticed he was counting the words he had written. Gerry asked Jarrod why he was doing that, and he replied, "Because we were told to write five hundred words and I am five short." When Gerry asked him what he was going to do, Jarrod said he would go back and include a few more "ands" or "thens" to make up the difference.

When checking the writing of your children in grades 4–8, you should look at the words they use to express their stories. Some students who write for length produce "safe spellings," that is, words they know how to spell and write. Figure 3.8 is a writing sample from a student in grade 8. This story used a total of 169 words; 3 of the words were invented, and 165 were conventional spellings. What does this tell us? This student used "safe" language resulting in a less than interesting story. Although he filled almost one page with text, the language he used was not consistent with the language development we would expect from a student in grade 8. This student would benefit from a thesaurus and from being taught how to substitute safe language with language that engages the readers or speaks directly to the intended audience. Children at this level should be using similes, metaphors, and personification (see glossary for definition) in their writing. Perhaps this could be discussed with the classroom teacher. By not demanding perfect spelling, children may be more willing to take risks and experiment with more sophisticated language.

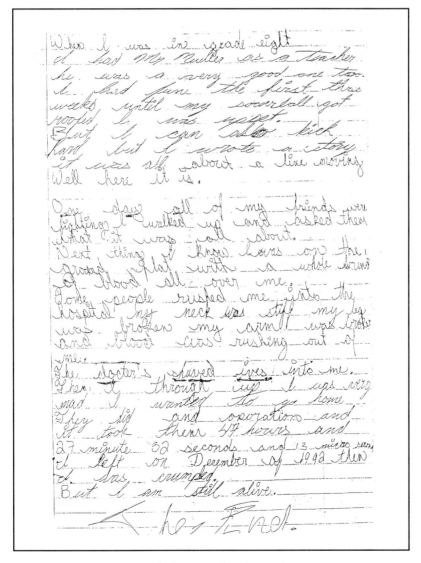

Figure 3.8. Writing sample from student in grade 8.

Memorization and Spelling

Parents frequently ask us about memorization and spelling. From their own school experiences, parents know that a spelling test was given at the end of the week to show the teacher which students could correctly spell their weekly words. The problem for many parents and teachers was trying to explain why children could spell words correctly on weekly spelling lessons and yet continue to spell those same words incorrectly when they write. From our perspective and based on what we know about the brain and memory, correct spelling involves internalization, not memorization. Words we are forced to memorize stay with us for only short periods of time, unless we use them on a regular basis. Allow us to demonstrate. Do the following activity (Bryson, 1990), but do not ask anyone for help and don't use a pencil to write the words out (we will explain why afterwards). We want you to rely on your memory and the knowledge you have about spelling.

Which of the following words are misspelled?

superced
conceed
procede
idiosyncracy
accomodate
dexterious
impressario
irresistable
rhythym
opthamologist
diptheria
anamoly
caesarin
grafitti

There are a total of fourteen words in the list. When asked how many of the words were spelled incorrectly we received a range of answers anywhere from five to ten. The answer is fourteen! Yes, all of the words are spelled incorrectly. (How did you do?) When we use this exercise with parents, we ask them to tell us what strategies they used to determine if the words were spelled correctly. Most parents said that their first reaction was to rely on sounding out. Since we had requested that you not ask anyone for help you could not confirm with others whether they were right or wrong. Also, we asked you not to use a pencil to write out the words. You had to use your knowledge about sounds and letters first. When you could not confirm your predictions by asking someone else, you probably wanted to write out the words to see if they looked right.

From Sounding Out to Visual Strategies

To illustrate how we shift from sounding out to visual strategies, we used the example of writing a letter or a note and wanting to write a word such as "accommodate" in a sentence. When you attempt to write the word and discover that you are not sure how to spell it you usually will try to sound it out. If this fails you move to a secondary visual strategy by going off the paper, writing options to determine if you can identify the word by the way it looks:

acomodate
acommodate
accomodate
accommodate

At this point learners shift from sounding out to visual strategies. With the word "accommodate" the problem is in determining the correct number of cs and ms. By writing the word, we visually reconstruct the word and make a prediction based on this information. Some people get to this point and want to be certain their guess is correct, so they rely on a textual source, such as a dictionary, to confirm their choice. Children are no different. We have come to view children as "survivors." In the interest of survival, they will manipulate two sources. The first source is human and the second source is textual. It is only natural to ask someone when you are not sure of the spelling of a word. Had you had access to dictionaries and thesauri when we first asked you to identify the correct spellings from the list, you would have scrambled to the dictionaries to confirm your predictions. By the way, the correct spellings for the fourteen words are

supersede/supercede
concede

proceed
idiosyncrasy
accommodate
dexterous
impresario
irresistible
rhythm
ophthalmologist
diphtheria
anomaly
cesarean
graffiti

There are many things that we commit to our memories, but a lot of this information is not stored in our brains through memorization. If this were the case, we would all be able to remember most of the information we had to learn when we wrote tests and exams during the school year. As the brain internalizes information, the information remains with us. What helps us to remember how to spell words? Is it frequency of use? Partly. The more we use something, the higher the chances that we will internalize the information. If we had worked for an ophthalmologist, we would have had no problem identifying an incorrect spelling. We were able to recognize the words; however, because we do not use many of them on a regular basis, identifying the correct spelling was difficult.

A little girl in Averil's kindergarten class, Mackayala, asked how to spell "meningitis." Since most five-year-olds ask her to spell words such as "Mom," "Dad," and "love" (all very important words to them), Averil was both surprised and curious. As the little girl laboriously printed the letters in her journal, she told Averil that her friend's father had died from meningitis. So it was an important word for her (as all of the hockey words had been to Nathan).

Two Types of Writing

When we work with teachers, we suggest that their writing and spelling programs address two components: personal writing and writing for publication. Most teachers teach writing as a process. The writing process is an approach that requires a piece of writing to go through several drafts—be edited and revised for the clarity of the intended message and liveliness of language, as well as for spelling, punctuation, and grammar. You might use this as a guide for writing at home or as an opportunity to meet with your child's teachers to find out how they handle their writing programs.

Personal Writing

The function of personal writing is to provide opportunities to write for enjoyment and self-expression, among other reasons. This type of writing does not go through editing and revision. Look for the changes in the words your child attempts to use (use the strategies discussed earlier). Anyone who shops for groceries knows that most of us use abbreviations (let/lettuce) and invented spellings (appls/apples) to help us remember what to buy. This is a form of personal writing that performs a function. Put a piece of paper on the refrigerator and invite your children to write down what they think you should buy when you go grocery shopping. Or better still, ask them to add things to the list for you. When they write words such as "lettuce," "carrot," "spaghetti," and so on, you will see what they know about spelling. Also, by allowing children to contribute items to the grocery list, you let them know that you value their input. Younger children will also feel successful when someone can interpret their first attempts at writing. Personal writing for children is no different. It can tell us an awful lot about their writing and spelling development.

Other forms of personal writing include signs and notes. Children love to make signs (see Figure 2.1, Greer's Sign to the Rest of the Family). They put them on their bedroom doors or post them throughout the house. Since Gerry often works at home, Jarrod decided to make a sign for his father's office door so that everyone would know not to disturb him (see Figure 3.9). Kids love to write notes to each other in school, but message writing can be done at home, too. You can set up a message board, where any message received or sent will be posted. Sticky notes are great for recording messages. Keep them by the telephone, in the kitchen, and in the kid's bedrooms. Messages are posted on the message board for everyone to see and respond to (see Figure 3.10).

Writing for Publication

A letter, a story, an editorial, thank you notes, invitations—any writing that your child may "publish" (that is, writing available for people to see and read) needs to have correct spelling and grammar. Teachers often refer to this form of writing as writing for publication. When children write for publication, they are taught to edit and revise their work so that the text flows and the message is clear. To edit and

Figure 3.9. Jarrod's sign for Dad's office.

Figure 3.10. A message board.

revise, young writers need competent writers to help them with spelling, punctuation, grammar, style, and usage. The more a beginning writer writes with an experienced writer the more she learns about language and all its structures and components.

There are two parts to editing and revision. The first is editing for meaning and clarity. This involves the child reading her work to someone in order to determine if the text sounds right or if any of the sentences are confusing or if the language is vague. Figure 3.11 is an example of a fourth-grade student's writing. We can see that this child uses common nouns to refer to events. For instance he refers to board games, a friend's house, an aunt's house, and buying clothes. These are examples of the vague language children use. To help them be more specific, teach them to look for vague language and to write in the actual names of people, places, and things—elements that add more detailed information to their stories. Encourage them to read their text to someone and ask that person to offer suggestions about vague language. Taking these suggestions, children can add more detail to their stories. Details help the reader of a story to interpret the text without wondering or questioning what the author was trying to say.

My Weekend

I went to my aunt's cottage. I played with my cousins and we watched a movie and played some board games. When I got home I went outside and played with my friends. My mom and dad took me out to buy some new clothes for school. My birthday is coming soon.

Figure 3.11. Writing sample from a student in grade 4.

Parent Story: Sharon Murphy, Detroit, Michigan

My daughter Njima is in grade 1 and was having problems at school with writing and spelling. I decided to have her write grocery lists as a way to help her overcome her fear of spelling and writing. Njima likes to draw and help out in the kitchen. The following occurred over a period of four weeks. When she started writing her first grocery list she drew pictures to support her writing (see Figure 3.12). She wrote large letters to go with her drawings. I did not say anything to Njima about the spelling, but I asked her to read her list to me and complimented her on her effort. To make this more meaningful, I took Njima to the grocery store. When we located an item on her list I calmly pointed out letters and moved on to the next isle. Three days later, Njima decided to make her second list (see Figure 3.13).

I could see that she was using mostly consonants that represented the names of the letters in the words. In some cases, she had the correct letters but in the wrong order (oil/oli). As we moved on to week two, Njima went into the kitchen to locate items for her list. I told her not to worry about misspelled words. What was visibly evident was Njima's desire to search for words and read. By now Njima felt comfortable making her lists and her third attempt shows how she was developing confidence in herself as a writer (see Figure 3.14).

Njima was very proud of herself and commented, "Now I do not need to go to the grocery store because you can read my list." On this attempt, Njima decided to number her list. She was proud of her list and her ability to find the words in the kitchen. For her final list (see Figure 3.15), Njima wrote twelve words and included "blue grass seed" because her father wanted to patch some areas in the lawn. Not all of her spellings are accurate, but I understand her development and that has taken the pressure off of us as her parents.

Figure 3.12. Njima's first grocery list.

Figure 3.13. Njima's second grocery list.

Figure 3.14. Njima's third grocery list.

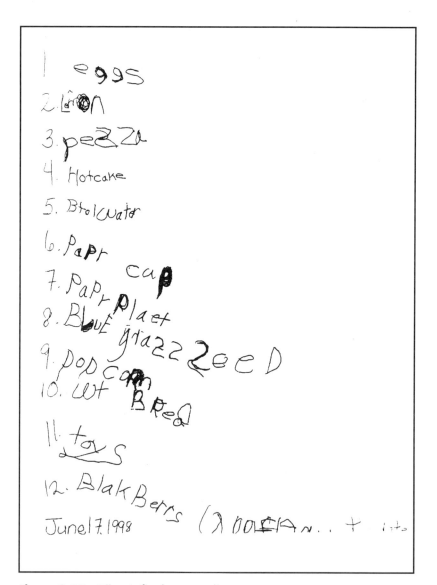

Figure 3.15. Njima's final grocery list.

Writing and Spelling Strategies to Use at Home

Word Webs

Use a pattern such as "sign" and try finding words that contain the pattern. The pattern can be at the beginning, middle, or end of a word (signal, signature, design, assignment). Encourage children to use prefixes and suffixes (redesign, designing, designed).

Word Power

Start with long words, for example, "encyclopedia." Invite your children to use the letters from this word to make as many other words as possible. Some examples from encyclopedia might be, cycle, dice, lay, once, lid, lion, and so on. Gerry's fourth grade class wrote 110 words using the letters from encyclopedia and at the same time provided him with information about their writing, spelling, and grammar.

Message Boards

Households are busy places. To help children value writing as a way to communicate, it would be helpful to establish a message board or message center in your house. Sometimes this can be the refrigerator door or a cupboard in the kitchen. You might even try a small bulletin board on which messages can be pinned. What works very well are "sticky notes." Depending on the number of adults and children in your household a section on the board can be allocated for certain individuals. Some parents just like to stick the notes in one area for everyone to read. Encourage your children to write down phone messages, where they are going after school, what time they want to get up, what they want for lunch, and so on. Most parents like to use the message board for phone messages; it has many other uses as well.

Note Writing

Children love to write notes to one another, and they really enjoy getting notes from their parents. Putting notes in lunch boxes can be a nice way to let your children know that you are thinking of them. It may be a "good luck" note for a test or exam, a part in a play or a sporting event they are in. Notes can be used at home. Communicate with your children when you want them to clean their room, take out the garbage, practice piano, or feed the dog. Notes can be left on the message board or in their rooms, on the refrigerator or by the telephone. The purpose of note writing is to demonstrate to your children that writing is a way to communicate. It also helps them to see how you spell certain words and use language to communicate. Buy and give sticky notes as gifts.

Grocery Lists

Writing grocery lists is a nice way to involve your children in making decisions about what is needed in the house. It also lets them experiment with a form of language they might not experience in schools. Place a piece of paper on the refrigerator (refrigerators seem to be a focal point in most households), keep a marker or pencil close by, and invite your children to write down things they think you need to buy when you go shopping. Don't insist on accuracy at first, but when the shopping is over, come back to the note and point out how they spelled the words and how the grocery store spells them. Look for changes each week.

Written Conversation

Written conversation is having a discussion on paper. You will need one piece of lined or blank paper. Tell your child that you are going to write her a question and then she is going to read the question, write an answer, and then write a question to you. You will then read her question, write an answer, and write another question. This exercise can go on for as long as you feel your child is enjoying the interaction. Written conversation is a nice way to communicate with your children and at the same time allows them to practice writing with an adult. This allows your children to access spelling and grammar from your writing that they might normally not use in school.

Sketch to Stretch

This activity uses art, instead of writing, to communicate ideas or feelings. Invite your children to draw or sketch a favorite part of a story that they read with you, or one that they read at school. When they finish, invite them to tell you about their drawing. This is a nice time to listen and discuss things such as characters, plot, setting, and endings. The key to the discussion is to ask questions, not to give answers. This way you are encouraging your children to use their ability to recall the events of the story from memory with help from their drawing.

Bookmarks

This activity is for children in grades 2 and up. Cut up pieces of paper similar in size to what a bookmark might look like. As your children read a story, invite them to use the bookmarks to write down for each page one thing they thought was an important event. They may also write down words they had difficulty with. After they have finished the book or the chapter, have them pull all of the bookmarks out of the book. Next, have them look at the bookmarks and describe to you the key events they wrote and why they thought they were important. You might also discuss any words with which they had difficulty. The bookmarks can be used to help them rewrite the story or can act as a good reference to write a book report.

Personal Dictionaries

Words children use on a regular basis can be put in a personal dictionary. A lined or blank book can be used to record words that children are learning to spell. They can include words from the kitchen, cereal boxes, environment, and so on. Have them print a letter at the top of each page so that the words are grouped together similar to a dictionary.

Journals

Give your child a notebook or diary so that she may record her thoughts. It is a good idea if you model this as well. To get her started, you might show her how you write in your own journal. It is crucial to remember that journals are private unless your child offers to read a passage to you. Since this is a journal of her favorite thoughts, don't place emphasis on spelling or grammar.

Commercial Games

Games such as Scrabble, Pictionary, Word Searches, Crosswords, and Boggle serve two purposes. First, they present language in a different context other than school, and second these games are highly social and can involve the entire family.

Technology

If you have a computer at home, there are a number of commercially produced software programs and CD ROM's (see Appendix A) available that support the development of written language and word awareness.

Reflections

It is difficult to put aside the rules we learned as children during our own schooling. Many parents are concerned about helping their children at home for fear of disrupting the program at school. We suggest that as parents you need to feel comfortable. It is important to remember that the time you invest

> **"My spelling is wobbly. It's good spelling but it wobbles and all the letters get in the wrong places."**
> **A. A. Milne (1926)**

with your children is what makes the difference in the long run. Take a few moments and write some questions about spelling and writing. Show this to your children and talk to them about what you are doing and why. Let them see you writing in this book so that they can appreciate that writing is not limited to students in schools and classrooms, but is used by parents as part of their learning.

Lingering Thoughts

4 Where to Begin

We would like for you to walk away with the idea that as parents we are also learners. Many studies of early readers show that children can and do learn to read at home without formal instruction. However, these children have almost always grown up in a literate environment in which books are valued and family members model reading and writing and in which children are read to frequently from a very early age. The key element in learning to read is a wide experience with books. When these experiences are not provided, four or five years of optimum learning time is lost. The sooner we start reading to children, the easier it is for reading to become an important part of their lives; the later we start, the more difficult it becomes. Although it is only the first step in many, developing and sustaining a love for books in our children is crucial. When children discover books and the joy they bring, they are on their way to becoming readers and writers.

Our children are constantly bombarded with print—on the roads, in restaurants, through mail and television advertising. Remember the stories of Jarrod and Kristin in the car? Children who come from literate homes quickly learn that printed messages have purpose and meaning. By providing their children with paper, crayons, pencils, and pens—along with a place to write and draw—parents send a strong message that this is part of learning, and it can be fun. And when children begin "writing," drawing, scribbling, invented letters, and spellings are legitimate forms of writing. Children should be encouraged and supported for their effort.

What Can We Do at Home?

The strategies we have mentioned throughout this book are only meant to provide you with the types of things you can do at home to help your children. You will have many more of your own ideas. We would like to offer a few ideas that we have tried in our homes.

- Make simple books with your child
- Make a family book together
- Let your child help you with the grocery list
- Play the alphabet game around the kitchen
- "Paint" words outside with water and brushes
- Visit the library on a regular basis
- Buy books in which children can write their names
- Buy magnetic letters for your refrigerator
- Play word games, such as Scrabble
- Leave messages on a message board
- Write notes to your children
- Label objects around the house together
- Write cards and letters together
- Send and read e-mail together

According to Jim Trelease (1995), if we want our children to become readers, we should remember the three B's.

1. Books
Buy books for your children. Let them print their names in them. Let them borrow books from the library, but also provide them with their own books. Purchase books at garage sales or let your child order books through book clubs. Take your children with you to buy books as birthday gifts when they attend birthday parties.

2. Baskets
Keep baskets of books and other types of print materials such as magazines and newspapers around the house, especially where family

members are often waiting. We all know about the bathroom (Averil and Gerry used books when their children were toilet training—it kept them occupied), but the kitchen can be a cozy spot too.

3. Bed Lights
Allow your readers to leave the light on after they have gone to bed. If you do not want lights on all night, just leave a hallway light on. Reading in dim light does not damage the eyes; it only makes them tired. There are also bulbs that gradually get dimmer. Reading by the light of a flashlight is fun, too.

Learning as a Social Process

Frank Smith (1992), who researches methods of teaching literacy, writes that learning depends on the company one keeps. What a powerful statement for this new millennium. If our children see teachers and parents working together to solve problems and deal with issues concerning children's literacy, surely this should demonstrate that problems are not obstacles to avoid or argue over, but rather, issues to be resolved together. Classrooms should reinforce this idea by allowing children the freedom to ask questions, offer an opinion, and comment on a range of issues. Given the diversity of cultures in our classrooms, learning from one another and about one another seems like a natural thing to do.

An Alphabet for Parents

Throughout this book, we have been talking about helping our children develop as readers and writers as they explore the English language. We would like to leave you with an alphabet of your own to think about.

A lways ask her what went well at school today.

B oast about the good things he tells me.

C elebrate her mistakes because everybody learns from mistakes.

D o a diary together—recounting family gatherings, outings, letters, and messages.

E ncourage him to be himself and to expect his very best.

F orget the adult worries and remember she's just a little girl.

G ather, go out and get experiences galore! Out of doing comes learning.

H ug him often—at least once every day (regardless of his size).

I nvite her to be the greatest, happiest child in the world. Tell her that and treat her accordingly.

J oin in when he's reading or studying, realizing that your actions speak louder than anything you can say.

K eep on learning yourself—all that you can see, do, and be—living life to its fullest.

L isten to her when she's troubled and laugh with her when she's joyous.

M ake a difference in his days by mentioning that you really care.

N otice when her hair is combed (at least when she comes down for breakfast).

O ffer him opportunities to decide things for himself—what to wear, when to do his chores; give him power over his life with all the risks that that entails.

P in up his artwork, tests, writings, heroes, and photographs, for all the family to enjoy (call up Grandma sometimes to remind her of his latest accomplishments).

Q uestion her teacher and her coaches often about how she feels she's doing at school and on her team.

R elax and enjoy childhood. Read to him often. Remember how fleeting are his childhood years.

S queeze praise into every day's time slots. Save a private moment for sharing what she chooses to share.

T urn the TV off sometimes to talk together—at the dinner table, before he goes to bed, when he comes in from little league.

U se her talents to the fullest. So that she realizes that her presence makes a difference to others, let her take out the garbage, wash the dishes, cook, and help at church or in the community.

V olunteer when needed? Be that model of helpfulness in school, demonstrating that learning is his and your most important business.

W ait patiently for her. She may be a late bloomer, a deep thinker, a slow mover.

X tra, extra, extra—that's what moms and dads are all about.

Y es, You are the one who counts. It's your values and strengths he will imitate.

Z oom ahead together in life, aware and confident that she is a unique gift to you.

Why not write some goals for yourself, or write a "to do" list. In closing, we would like to end with an invitation to you. If this book has helped you in some small way, please feel free to write to us and tell us of your accomplishments. Or maybe you have a question to which you cannot find an answer and with which we may be able to help you. We have provided you with addresses, phone numbers, and e-mail locations where we can be contacted. Above all, remember that growth takes time; however, it only happens when you become involved.

Reflections: Some Final Thoughts about Family Literacy

In closing, we feel a need to share our feelings about educational change and what it means for parents. Whether you live in Detroit, Michigan; San Diego, California; or Windsor, Ontario, picking up a newspaper and finding an article about education (good or bad) is not difficult. Research strongly suggests that when parents get involved in their children's education literacy rates increase. Parents want their children to succeed. Now, more than ever, education is looking at parenting and learning in the home as a way to view literacy. The home is a natural place where all subjects and content exist. The movement toward more parental involvement suggests that if educators and parents combine their collective knowledge, our children's literacy will have no boundaries. It is becoming more evident that the home curriculum must work in conjunction with the school curriculum.

Lingering Thoughts

_____

_____

_____

_____

_____

_____

_____

_____

_____

Appendix A: Annotated Bibliography of Children's Literature

This listing of children's literature is provided as a resource to teachers who are interested in finding appropriate books for the children in their classrooms. This is, of course, not an exhaustive list. The books were selected from lists of award-winning children's books, from favorite choices of children, and from books the authors have successfully used in their work with children. Particular attention was paid to books that a large number of children could relate to and that were sensitive to the interests and needs of children at the specific grade level.

The books are organized according to grade levels. Readability was established in a variety of ways. Fry's readability formula (1977) was used to establish a base level. However, the books were also examined for repetitive lines and phrases, familiar concepts for the age group, and high interest level, all of which can influence the readability of any text. These readability groupings are meant only as a guideline. Children should be encouraged to read and work with a variety of levels of materials.

This bibliography is reprinted from *Classroom Assessment of Reading Processes* (1997) by Diane Allen and Rebecca Swearingen.

First Grade

1. **Ahlberg, Janet, & Ahlberg, Allan.** *Each Peach Pear Plum.* New York: Viking Kestrel, 1978. 28 pages (unpaged).

   This easy rhyming book invites the readers to participate by giving them something to look for in each picture. All clues are related to famous fairy tale and nursery rhyme characters such as Cinderella, Old Mother Hubbard, and the Three Bears.

2. **Aliki.** *We Are Best Friends.* New York: Mulberry Books, 1982. 28 pages (unpaged).

   Peter and Robert are best friends, but Peter is moving away. At first Robert is lonely and sad. A new boy, Will, moves to Robert's neighborhood and they discover that new friends can be found.

3. **Asch, Frank.** *Happy Birthday, Moon.* Upper Saddle River, NJ: Prentice-Hall, 1982. 28 pages (unpaged).

   Bear decides to give Moon a birthday present. He is excited to find out that he and Moon share the same birthday. Bear takes all of the money in his piggy bank and buys Moon a hat. What a surprise: Moon gives Bear an identical hat.

4. **Bennett, Jill.** *Teeny Tiny.* Illustrated by Tomie dePaola. New York: Trumpet Club, 1985. 28 pages (unpaged).

   A teeny tiny woman finds a teeny tiny bone in the graveyard. She takes the bone home to make soup. Before she makes the soup, she decides to take a nap. She is tormented by a voice asking for the bone. Finally, the teeny tiny woman tells the voice to take the bone.

5. **Brown, Margaret W.** *The Runaway Bunny.* Illustrated by Clement Hurd. New York: Harper & Row, 1970. 33 pages (unpaged).

   In this perennial favorite, Little Bunny tries to think of ways to run away from his mother. His mother always thinks of ways she could find him. In the end, Little Bunny decides he may as well stay at home.

6. **Carle, Eric.** *The Very Busy Spider.* New York: Philomel Books, 1984. 22 pages (unpaged).

   A spider lands on a farmyard fence and begins to weave her web. Various farm animals try to distract her, but she stays with the spinning until it is finished. At the end of the day, the farm animals realize what a beautiful thing a web is. The repetitive line helps make this an easy reader.

7. **Carle, Eric.** *The Very Hungry Caterpillar.* New York: Philomel Books, 1987. 22 pages (unpaged).

   On a Sunday morning, a very hungry caterpillar hatches from a tiny egg on a leaf. He eats his way through the week. By the end of the week, he is a very fat caterpillar. He builds a cocoon around himself. When he emerges, he is a beautiful butterfly. Children love the actual "holes" the caterpillar eats through food in this book. The book is useful in studying the days of the week, the metamorphosis of caterpillars, and counting.

8. **Christopher, Matt.** *The Dog That Pitched a No-Hitter.* Illustrated by Daniel Vasconcellos. New York: Trumpet Club, 1988. 42 pages.

   Mike and his dog, Harry, have a special relationship: they can read each other's minds. Harry loves and knows baseball. He helps Mike pitch a no-hitter game.

9. **Cohen, Miriam.** *No Good in Art.* Illustrated by Lillian Hoban. New York: Dell Publishing, 1980. 29 pages (unpaged).

   In kindergarten, Jim's art teacher does not like his paintings because he forgets to give his men necks, and he makes his grass too fat. In first grade, Jim's class has a new art teacher. She tells the class to paint pictures of what they want to be when they grow up. Jim does not want to paint because he does not think he can. The art teacher persuades him to paint something he likes to do. Everyone in the class loves Jim's work, and he decides maybe he can do art.

10. **Fox, Mem.** *Hattie and the Fox.* Illustrated by Patricia Mullins. New York: Trumpet Club, 1986. 16 pages (unpaged).

    Hattie sees something suspicious in the bushes and tries to alert the other farm animals. No one particularly cares until the fox jumps out of the bushes.

11. **Galbraith, Kathryn O.** *Look! Snow!* Illustrated by Nina Montezimos. New York: Margaret K. McElderry Books, 1992. 27 pages (unpaged).

The limited text is supplemented by wonderful pictures. Children can use these pictures to tell their own stories of a snow day away from school.

12. **Giff, Patricia R.** *Spectacular Stone Soup.* Illustrated by Blanche Sims. New York: Dell Publishing, 1989. 76 pages.

Mrs. Zachary, Stacy Arrow's teacher, likes for her students to be people-helpers. Stacy wants to be a people-helper, but her good efforts backfire every time. Finally, Stacy learns what helping people is all about when she contributes to the class's spectacular stone soup.

13. **Giff, Patricia R.** *The Valentine Star.* Illustrated by Blanche Sims. New York: Dell Publishing, 1985. 72 pages.

Emily starts a feud with Sherri that threatens to ruin her entire year in school. Each one tries to do something worse to the other. A student teacher finally resolves the situation by enlisting their help in a joint project to create a card for their regular teacher.

14. **Hughes, Shirley.** *Bouncing.* Cambridge, MA: Candlewick Press, 1993. 16 pages (unpaged).

This book looks at all the ways children can bounce—on a bed, on a sofa, on pillows, etc. Children enjoy the humor and fun depicted in the beautiful pictures.

15. **Kalen, Robert.** *Jump Frog, Jump.* Illustrated by Byron Barton. New York: Mulberry Books, 1981. 30 pages (unpaged).

This cumulative story draws children in with its repetitive line, "Jump frog, jump." Frog escapes many dangers in the pond until he is captured by some young boys. Frog's only escape is to "Jump frog, jump!"

16. **Kraus, Robert.** *Leo the Late Bloomer.* Illustrated by Jose Aruego. New York: Crowell, 1971. 28 pages (unpaged).

   Leo's father is worried because Leo can't read, write, or speak. His mother is not worried because she knows that Leo is just a late bloomer. Leo's father watches and watches for Leo to bloom. Leo finally blooms in his own way and time.

17. **Lobel, Arnold.** *Owl at Home.* New York: Harper & Row, 1975. 64 pages.

   This easy chapter book shares Owl's experiences at home—for example, an uninvited guest, bumps in his bed, the making of tear-water tea, and becoming friends with the moon.

18. **Martin, Bill.** *Brown Bear, Brown Bear, What Do You See?* Illustrated by Eric Carle. Austin, TX: Holt, Rinehart & Winston, 1983. 24 pages (unpaged).

   This is a repetitive chant in which one animal asks another what he sees. The rhythm and repetition provide for a fun read-aloud. Color words and words that follow basic word patterns make this an easy reader.

19. **Mayer, Mercer.** *Was So Mad.* Racine, WI: Western Publishing Co., 1983. 23 pages (unpaged).

   Monster was so mad because he could not do what he wanted. He packs his things to run away until his friends invite him to go to the park. He decides to run away tomorrow.

20. **Minarik, Else Holmelund.** *A Kiss for Little Bear.* Illustrated by Maurice Sendak. New York: Trumpet Club, 1988. 32 pages.

   Hen takes a picture to Grandmother for Little Bear. Grandmother asks Hen to thank Little Bear for the gift by giving him a kiss. On her way back to Little Bear, Hen asks various forest creatures to pass the kiss on.

21. **Minarik, Else Holmelund.** *Little Bear.* Illustrated by Maurice Sendak. New York: Trumpet Club, 1988. 63 pages.

   This simple chapter book for young readers details several episodes in Little Bear's life. In the chapter "What Will Little Bear Wear?"

Little Bear continuously asks Mother Bear for something additional to wear because he is so cold. In "Birthday Soup" Little Bear is convinced that Mother Bear has forgotten his birthday. He prepares birthday soup for his friends who arrive to help him celebrate. Little Bear realizes that Mother Bear has not forgotten his birthday when she arrives with the birthday cake. The third chapter, "Little Bear Goes to the Moon," tells the story of what happens to Little Bear when he decides that he can fly to the moon. The final chapter, "Little Bear's Wish," brings closure to the book by summarizing all of Little Bear's adventures.

22. **Numeroff, Laura J.** *If You Give a Mouse a Cookie.* Illustrated by Felicia Bond. New York: Scholastic Inc., 1985. 28 pages (unpaged).

What happens when you offer a cookie to a mouse? Lots of things. In fact, the mouse will take over your home and one thing leads to another. This is a fun, rhythmic story that children find wonderfully humorous.

23. **Rylant, Cynthia.** *Henry and Mudge and the Wild Wind.* Illustrated by Sucie Stevenson. New York: Trumpet Club, 1993. 40 pages.

Henry is afraid of thunderstorms, but Mudge is even more afraid. He circles the kitchen table, hides his head in the couch cushions, or sits in the bathroom. During one storm, Henry's parents try to keep Henry entertained with games and food. It works for Henry but not for Mudge.

24. **Stevenson, James.** *Quick! Turn the Page!* New York: Greenwillow Books, 1990. 29 pages (unpaged).

The repetitive phrase keeps children turning the pages of this easy reader. The teacher has many opportunities to engage students in predicting what will be on the next page.

25. **Wood, Audrey.** *The Napping House.* Illustrated by Don Wood. Orlando, FL: Harbrace Juvenile Books, 1984. 29 pages (unpaged).

This is a cumulative tale of a napping granny who is joined in her nap by a child, a dog, a cat, a mouse, and a flea. The result is hilarious. Children enjoy the repetition. The pictures are breathtaking.

Second Grade

1. **Adler, David A.** *Cam Jansen and the Mystery of the Stolen Diamonds.* Illustrated by Susanna Natti. New York: Viking Press, 1980. 58 pages.

   Cam Jansen and her friend Eric Shelton are sitting in the mall watching Eric's baby brother when they hear the alarm go off in the jewelry store. They witness a man run from the store and through the mall. Cam and Eric follow the man and discover who really committed the crime.

2. **Allard, Harry, & Marshall, James.** *Miss Nelson Has a Field Day.* Boston: Houghton Mifflin. 1985. 32 pages.

   The children in Horace B. Smedley School are depressed because their football team is awful. The team will not listen to the coach. When the coach is absent for a few days, Viola Swamp appears and whips the team into shape. They win the big game with the Central Werewolves. The surprise in this book is that Miss Nelson has a twin.

3. **Allard, Harry, & Marshall, James.** *Miss Nelson Is Missing.* Boston: Houghton Mifflin. 1982. 32 pages.

   When Miss Nelson has her tonsils out, Mr. Blandsworth, the principal, substitutes. He is so boring that the children develop a plan to convince him that Miss Nelson is back. Miss Nelson stops the class's fun when she becomes Viola Swamp, their new substitute. The children are truly glad when Miss Nelson returns.

4. **Brown, Marc.** *Arthur's Nose.* New York: Trumpet Club. 1976. 28 pages (unpaged).

   Arthur is unhappy with his nose, so he decides to change it. The doctor asks Arthur to try on pictures of noses of other animals to select the one he wants. Arthur discovers that he likes his own nose best.

5. **Calmenson, Stephanie.** *The Principal's New Clothes.* Illustrated by Denise Brunkus. New York: Scholastic Inc., 1989. 36 pages (unpaged).

This is a modern version of *The Emperor's New Clothes*. In this case, Mr. Bundy, the principal, is tricked by a couple who promise to make him a one-of-a-kind new suit. Only smart people and people who are doing their jobs well can see the new suit. An honest kindergarten student helps the principal face the truth.

6. **Cleary, Beverly.** *Two Dog Biscuits.* Illustrated by DyAnne DiSalvo-Ryan. New York: Dell Publishing, 1961. 30 pages (unpaged).

   Jimmy and Janet are twins. Their neighbor, Mrs. Robbins, gives each twin a dog biscuit. Their mother takes them on a walk to find a dog who might want the dog biscuits. However, the twins cannot find a dog that they want to have the biscuits. They decide, instead, to give their dog biscuits to a cat.

7. **Cleary, Beverly.** *Janet's Thingamajigs.* Illustrated by DyAnne DiSalvo-Ryan. New York: William Morrow & Co., 1987. 30 pages (unpaged).

   Janet and Jimmy are twins. Janet loves to collect little things, "thingamajigs," put them in brown paper bags, and put them in her crib. Jimmy wants Janet to share, but she refuses. Mother does not know what to do. One day she surprises the twins with new beds. Janet's thingamajigs will not stay on the new beds, so she decides they are not important anymore.

8. **Cushman, Doug.** *Aunt Eater's Mystery Vacation.* New York: HarperCollins, 1992. 64 pages.

   Aunt Eater goes on a vacation to Hotel Bathwater. While on vacation, she is called on to solve three mysteries. All she really wants to do is read her mystery book. In the end, she meets the author of her favorite books.

9. **dePaola, Tomie.** *Oliver Button Is a Sissy.* Illustrated by the author. Orlando, FL: Harcourt Brace, 1979. 43 pages (unpaged).

   Oliver Button does not like to do the things that other little boys like to do. His father wants him to play ball, but he is too clumsy. His parents decide to let him go to dancing school for the exercise. The boys at school make fun of Oliver every day. Oliver participates in a talent show, and the other kids realize that he is a star.

10. **Freeman, Don.** *Corduroy.* Illustrated by the author. New York: Scholastic Inc., 1968. 32 pages.

    Corduroy is a little stuffed bear who lives in a department store. He dreams of a home of his own. One day a little girl sees Corduroy in the store and wants to buy him. At first her mother refuses, but she finally allows the little girl to use her savings to buy Corduroy.

11. **Hoban Russell.** *A Bargain for Frances.* Illustrated by Lillian Hoban. New York: Scholastic Inc., 1970. 63 pages.

    Frances wants a new china tea set with blue pictures painted on it. Her friend Thelma convinces her that such a tea set is unavailable, and that Frances should buy Thelma's plastic tea set instead. Frances later learns that Thelma takes the money and buys herself the china tea set. Frances successfully changes the situation to her favor.

12. **Hughes, Shirley.** *The Snow Lady.* New York: Lothrop, Lee & Shepard Books, 1990. 24 pages (unpaged).

    Sam lives on Trotter Street next door to Mrs. Dean. Mrs. Dean is always stopping Sam and her dog, Mick, or her friends from playing. They call her Mrs. Mean. After the first snowfall, Sam and her friend Barney build a snowlady and name her Mrs. Mean. Luckily the rain washes it away before Mrs. Dean can see it.

13. **Lawlor, Laurie.** *Second-Grade Dog.* Illustrated by Gioia Fiammenghi. Morton Grove, IL: Albert Whitman & Co., 1990. 37 pages (unpaged).

    Bones is a lucky dog; he has everything a dog could want. But Bones wants to go to school. He searches through the attic and finds clothes that he hopes will disguise him as a little boy. The next day he joins the second grade. The children realize he's a dog, but the teachers and principal do not notice until a fire fighter points it out. Bones is not allowed to return to school, but his new friends promise to visit him every day.

14. **Lobel, Arnold.** *Frog and Toad Together.* New York: Harper & Row, 1972. 64 pages.

This easy chapter book details the daily activities of two friends, Frog and Toad. In Chapter 1, "A List," Toad makes a to-do list for the day and marks off activities as they are completed. In Chapter 2, "The Garden," Frog helps Toad grow a flower garden. Chapter 3, "Cookies," finds the two friends trying to develop will power so they won't eat too many cookies. In Chapter 4, "Dragons and Giants," Frog and Toad prove they are brave. In Chapter 5, "The Dream," Toad dreams that Frog goes away.

15. **Pickett, Anola.** *Old Enough for Magic.* Illustrated by Ned Delaney. New York: HarperTrophy, 1989. 64 pages.

Peter gets a magic set for his birthday. His sister, Arlene, accidentally turns herself into a frog because she fails to read the directions. Peter asks everyone he meets how they solve problems. By following their advice, he is able to undo the spell.

16. **Porte, Barbara S.** *Harry's Birthday.* Illustrated by Yossi Abolafia. New York: Greenwillow Books, 1994. 47 pages.

Harry's birthday is coming up. He's wishing for a cowboy hat. His dad will not hire a clown or take the guests to get pizza. Harry settles for cake and ice cream at home. Uncle Leo and Aunt Rose provide the entertainment. All the guests have a great time, and Harry gets his wish—seven cowboy hats!

17. **Rodgers, Frank.** *Doodle Dog.* New York: Dutton, 1990. 29 pages (unpaged).

Sam wants a dog, but his mother says he cannot have one in an apartment. She and Sam draw a picture of a dog. Sam names him Doodle. In Sam's imagination Doodle becomes alive, and they share an adventurous trip to a farm.

18. **Rylant, Cynthia.** *Henry and Mudge and the Best Day of All.* Illustrated by Sucie Stevenson. New York: Trumpet Club, 1995. 40 pages.

It's May 1 and Henry's birthday. Henry has a party and invites all his friends. Mother and Father have set up games such as ringtoss, potato sack races, and a piñata in the backyard. After playing the games, the children eat cake and ice cream and watch Henry open his gifts. It's the best day of the year.

19. **Rylant, Cynthia.** *Miss Maggie.* Illustrated by Thomas DiGrazia. New York: Dutton, 1983. 26 pages (unpaged).

   Maggie Ziegler, an old woman, lives next to Nat Crawford's farm. Although Nat goes to Miss Maggie's house often, he never goes in because he has heard that she keeps a snake hanging from the rafters. The two become close friends after Nat rescues Miss Maggie from a very cold cabin with no fire.

20. **Sendak, Maurice.** *Where the Wild Things Are.* Illustrated by the author. New York: Harper & Row, 1963. 37 pages (unpaged).

   Max's mother calls him a "wild thing" and sends him to his room. Max travels to the land of the wild things but returns to find supper waiting for him.

21. **Sharmant, Marjorie W.** *Nate the Great and the Mushy Valentine.* Illustrated by Marc Simont. New York: Bantam Doubleday Dell Publishing Group, 1994. 44 pages.

   In this easy chapter book, Nate the Great has two mysteries to solve. Who sent the mushy valentine to Sludge, his dog? Who stole the valentine that Annie was making? After collecting all the clues, Nate the Great solves the mystery in his usual, careful manner.

22. **Sharmant, Marjorie W.** *Nate the Great and the Sticky Case.* Illustrated by Marc Simont. New York: Dell Publishing, 1978. 48 pages.

   Claude has lost his favorite stegosaurus stamp, and he wants Nate to solve the mystery. Annie, Rosamond, and Pip were at Claude's house right before the disappearance. Nate determines that the stamp must have stuck to the bottom of Pip's rain-soaked shoes. Unfortunately the shoes have been traded and sold a number of times. Nate follows the trail and solves the mystery.

23. **Sharmant, Marjorie W., & Weinman, Rosalind.** *Nate the Great and the Pillowcase.* Illustrated by Marc Simont. New York: Bantam Doubleday Dell Publishing Group, 1993. 48 pages.

   Rosamond calls Nate the Great in the middle of the night to tell him that the pillowcase that her cat, Big Hex, sleeps on is missing. Because Nate is a serious detective, he throws on his bathrobe and proceeds to investigate the mystery. After talking with Annie, Rosamond's friend, Nate the Great solves the mystery and returns home to bed.

24. **Turner, Ann.** *Sewing Quilts.* Illustrated by Thomas B. Allen. New York: Macmillan, 1994. 28 pages (unpaged).

    This book shares the heritage one little girl gets from her mother's quilting. The little girl and her sister begin their own quilts. Soft pictures add to the warm feeling from this book.

25. **Viorst, Judith.** *Alexander and the Terrible, Horrible, No Good, Very Bad Day.* Illustrated by Ray Cruz. New York: Antheneum, 1972. 28 pages (unpaged).

    Alexander's day is a disaster from the beginning when he wakes up with gum in his hair. Kids can identify with the "catastrophes" in Alexander's day. In the end, Alexander realizes that some days are just meant to be bad.

Third Grade

1. **Adler, David A.** *Cam Jansen and the Mystery of the Stolen Corn Popper.* Illustrated by Susanna Natti. New York: Viking Penguin, 1986. 58 pages.

   Cam Jansen and her best friend, Eric Shelton, go to Binky's Department Store to shop for school supplies. The store is very crowded because Binky's is having big sales in every department. While they are shopping, they are witness to the theft of several shopping bags. Cam, with her photographic memory, and Eric set about to solve the mystery.

2. **Baker, Barbara.** *Third Grade Is Terrible.* Illustrated by Roni Shepherd. New York: Dutton, 1989. 106 pages.

   Liza knows that third grade will be wonderful because she has been assigned to Mrs. Lane's room. Her reassignment to Mrs. Rumford's room is only one of many things that go wrong. Her best friend makes friends with someone else, she has no friends in Mrs. Rumford's class, and Amy Cutter, Miss Perfect, sits right in

front of her. Through all of her trials during the first week of
school, Liza finally makes friends with a new girl and mends her
relationship with her best friend.

3. **Blume, Judy.** *Freckle Juice.* Old Tappan, NJ: Four Winds Press,
   1971. 40 pages.

   Andrew Marcus wants to have freckles just like Nicky Lane. Sharon
   sells him a secret formula for freckle juice for fifty cents. The
   concoction makes Andrew sick, and he realizes that Sharon has
   tricked him. When he returns to school, he puts blue marks on his
   face and tells the class that the formula gave him blue freckles.
   Miss Kelly has a magic formula, and Andrew uses it to rid himself
   of his freckles.

4. **Bunting, Eve.** *Fly Away Home.* Illustrated by Ronald Himler.
   Boston: Clarion Books, 1991. 32 pages.

   Andrew and his father have been homeless since Andrew's mother
   died. They live at the airport. Andrew works hard at not being
   noticed because they would have to leave the airport. He hopes
   that one day his father will be able to find them a place to live.

5. **Bunting, Eve.** *Night Tree.* Illustrated by Ted Rand. New York:
   Trumpet Club, 1991. 28 pages (unpaged).

   A little boy with his father, mother, and sister, Nina, look for their
   tree on Christmas Eve. Instead of cutting it down, they decorate it
   with seeds, popcorn chains, and fruit for the creatures of the
   forest. After decorating the tree, they sit under the moonlit sky
   and sing favorite Christmas songs. This is an especially beautiful
   story for the holiday season because it deals with the joys of
   giving.

6. **Catling, Patrick S.** *The Chocolate Touch.* Illustrated by Margot
   Apple. New Brighton: Bantam, 1952. 87 pages.

   This older book is still delightful. John Midas loves candy better
   than anything, and his favorite candy is chocolate. He discovers a
   unique coin and an unusual candy store. He spends the coin to
   buy a box of chocolate. After eating the chocolate, John discovers
   that everything he puts into his mouth turns to chocolate. At first

he is thrilled, but his excitement is short lived. John learns his lesson about being selfish and greedy, and his life returns to normal.

7. **Cleary, Beverly.** *Ellen Tebbits.* New York: Bantam Doubleday Dell Publishing Group, 1979. 160 pages.

   Ellen Tebbits and Austine Allen become best friends in third grade. They share ballet, horseback riding, and a terrible secret—their mothers make them wear long woolen underwear. On the first day of fourth grade, Ellen slaps her best friend and is miserable until she figures out a way to say she's sorry.

8. **Cleary, Beverly.** *Muggie Maggie.* New York: Avon Books, 1990. 70 pages.

   Maggie Schultz's third grade teacher tells them that this will be a wonderful year. Maggie is doubtful because she dreads cursive writing. The grown-ups in her life do not understand her reluctance to write. Their pressure forces Maggie to vow to herself that she will never write cursive. Only Maggie can decide when the time is right to learn this new skill.

9. **Dahl, Roald.** *The Enormous Crocodile.* New York: Bantam, 1988. 42 pages.

   The Enormous Crocodile is hungry for children. As he walks through the jungle to the village, he tells his plans to several of the jungle inhabitants. In the village, the Enormous Crocodile attempts to implement his various plans for catching children. Each time he is thwarted by one of the jungle beasts he had met on his journey. The elephant flings the Enormous Crocodile into outer space, where he collides with the sun.

10. **dePaola, Tomie.** *The Legend of the Bluebonnet.* Illustrated by the author. New York: G. P. Putnam, 1983. 27 pages (unpaged).

    The People have been suffering from drought and famine. The Great Spirits say that an offering of the most valued possession is the only way to stop the drought. She-Who-Is-Alone gives up her warrior doll, the only thing she has left to remind her of her family. As a reward, the Great Spirits cover the hillsides with bluebonnets and end the drought.

11. **Duffey, Betsy.** *How to Be Cool in the Third Grade.* Illustrated by Janet Wilson. New York: Trumpet Club, 1993. 69 pages.

    Bobbie York wants to be "cool" for the first day of third grade. Unfortunately his day gets off to a bad start. He has to wear shorts instead of the jeans he's sure everyone else will be wearing. His mother walks him to the bus stop and gives him a big kiss before he gets on the bus. Then Robbie trips on the bus and lands in the lap of the school bully, Bo Haney. The worst part of the day is when Robbie finds out that he has to be a reading buddy to Bo Haney, who is assigned to the same third grade classroom. Robbie resolves to change some of these things so he can be cool. He learns that the changes are not that difficult but also that being cool is not the most important thing in life.

12. **Fleischman, Paul.** *Time Train.* Illustrated by Claire Ewart. New York: Trumpet Club, 1991. 29 pages (unpaged).

    Miss Pym's students are riding a train to Dinosaur National Monument to study dinosaurs over spring break. This is a very unusual train. By the time they arrive at the park, they have traveled millions of years back in time to the age of dinosaurs. They are able to study dinosaurs in very real settings. The author, however, includes some unrealistic activities, such as playing football, with the dinosaurs as well. All too soon, their time is up and they travel the time train back to reality.

13. **Fleischman, Sid.** *The Case of the 264-Pound Burglar.* Illustrated by Bill Morrison. New York: Random House, 1982. 62 pages.

    The Bloodhouse Gang is called in to solve the mystery of Mrs. Tolliver's missing money. They investigate evidence at the scene and narrow the suspects to twin nephews of Mrs. Tolliver.

14. **Friedman, Tracy.** *Henriette: The Story of a Doll.* Illustrated by Vera Rosenberry. New York: Scholastic Inc., 1986. 63 pages.

    Henriette is a porcelain doll who has belonged to three generations of little girls. She has never met her current owner, and she feels she must travel the long distance to Atlanta to find her owner, who lives in an orphanage. This book details the incredible efforts of the doll as she endures dangers and unruly children.

15. Gondosch, Linda. *The Monsters of Marble Avenue.* Illustrated by Cat Bowman Smith. New York: Little, Brown, 1988. 60 pages.

Luke Palmer has a big problem. He has promised to do a puppet show for Erin Bozwell's birthday party, but his mother sold all of his puppets at a garage sale. Luke's friends help him make some new puppets and then help him put on the puppet show.

16. Hoffman, Mary. *Amazing Grace.* Illustrated by Caroline Binch. New York: Dial Books for Young Readers, 1991. 24 pages (unpaged).

Grace loves stories, and she loves to act them out. Grace's teacher announces that the class will be doing the play *Peter Pan,* and Grace decides to try out for the lead. Her classmates tell her she cannot play Peter Pan because she is a girl and because she is black. Grace practices and practices for the part. Her hard work pays off when she lands the lead.

17. Johnson, Paul B. *The Cow Who Wouldn't Come Down.* Illustrated by the author. New York: Trumpet Club, 1993. 28 pages (unpaged).

Miss Rosemary's cow, Gertrude, decides to become a flying cow. Nothing that Miss Rosemary does persuades Gertrude to come back down and act like a normal cow. Miss Rosemary places a sign advertising for a new cow on her gate. The next morning a "new" cow appears. This brings Gertrude back to the ground in a hurry. What will she think of next? The author gives a pictorial hint that will encourage children to compose a sequel.

18. Kerby, Mona. *38 Weeks Till Summer Vacation.* New York: Scholastic, Inc., 1989. 90 pages.

With Mrs. Carter as her teacher, Nora Jean is sure that fourth grade will be lots of fun. Unfortunately Jimmy Lee Drover, the school bully, has also been assigned to her class. Despite Jimmy Lee's constant harassment, Nora Jean has a good year. She and Jimmy Lee even become friends in the end.

19. MacLachlan, Patricia. *Sarah, Plain and Tall.* New York: Harper/ Trophy, 1985. 58 pages. Newbery winner.

After Anna and Caleb's mother dies, their father advertises for a wife and mother. Sarah, a native of Maine, applies by writing letters to Anna, Caleb, and their father. After Sarah arrives at their prairie home, Anna and Caleb learn to love their new mother.

20. **MacLachlan, Patricia.** *Three Names.* Illustrated by Alexander Pertzoff. New York: HarperCollins, 1991. 31 pages.

This is the story of Grandfather and his dog, Three Names. Three Names goes to the prairie school with Grandfather. The story describes what one-room schools were like during the first part of this century.

21. **Markham, Marion M.** *The April Fool's Day Mystery.* Illustrated by Paul Estrada. Gainesville, FL: Camelot Books, 1991. 58 pages.

Mickey and Kate Dixon are twins, and they like to solve mysteries. Mickey is a detective, and Kate is a scientist. In this book they have to find out who put a snake in the cafeteria's flour bin. Everyone suspects Billy Wade, but the twins find evidence to the contrary.

22. **Myers, Bernice.** *Sidney Rella and the Glass Sneaker.* New York: Macmillan, 1985. 30 pages (unpaged).

In this modern version of Cinderella, a young boy is ridiculed and made to work by his two mean brothers. What Sidney really wants to do is play football. His fairy godfather grants him his wish, but Sidney must be home by six o'clock. Sidney wins the game but has to leave before receiving his trophy. The coach goes door to door to locate the boy who can wear the glass sneaker. Sidney becomes famous and grows up to own his own company.

23. **Myers, Laurie.** *Garage Sale Fever.* Illustrated by Kathleen Collins Howell. New York: HarperCollins, 1993. 86 pages.

Will decides to have a garage sale after the contents of his closet fall on top of him and almost injure his dog. Once the word gets around school, all of his friends want to participate. The garage sale is a success until Will's friend Pete sells a gift he received from Louise to her best friend, Jan. Jan plans to give the gift to Louise for her birthday. Will's solution to the problem is brilliant.

24. **Naylor, Phyllis R.** *One of the Third Grade Thonkers.* Illustrated by Walter Gaffney-Kessell. New York: Antheneum, 1988. 136 pages.

    Jimmy Novak, Sam Angelino, and Peter Nilsson are Thonkers. Thonkers have proven their bravery in outstanding ways such as living through operations, bone breaks, and car wrecks. When Jimmy's young cousin comes to stay with Jimmy's family when his mother has heart surgery, Jimmy learns a new meaning of bravery.

25. **Steig, William.** *Sylvester and the Magic Pebble.* New York: Trumpet Club, 1969. 30 pages (unpaged). Caldecott winner.

    Sylvester Duncan collects unusual pebbles. One day he finds a magic pebble. Unfortunately, he runs into a lion and wishes to himself that he was a rock. Unable to touch the stone and wish himself normal, Sylvester has to stay as a rock. His parents, on a picnic the following spring, find the magic pebble and Sylvester is rescued.

Fourth Grade

1. **Blume, Judy.** *Here's to You, Rachel Robinson.* New York: Dell Publishing, 1993. 196 pages.

   Rachel's big brother is expelled from boarding school and is causing a lot of worries for Rachel and her friends. Although Rachel is a straight A student, she still has many problems: seventh grade, boys, her sister's problems, but mostly her brother.

2. **Blume, Judy.** *Are You There God? It's Me, Margaret.* New York: Dell Publishing, 1970. 149 pages.

   After moving from New York City, Margaret finds everything different. She makes some very good friends with whom she can share personal things. But can she tell them she has no religion? Everyone belongs to a Jewish "Y," one of her friends is Catholic, but what is she? So Margaret asks God for help.

3. **Blume, Judy.** *Iggie's House.* New York: Dell Publishing, 1970. 117 pages.

   Winnie's best friend, Iggie, moves away, and a new family has moved into the house. Winnie hopes they will be as good as friends as she and Iggie were. The family is the only black family on the block. Will this be a problem for Winnie?

4. **Blume, Judy.** *Starring Sally J. Freeman as Herself.* New York: Dell Publishing, 1977. 298 pages.

   In the time of World War II, ten-year-old Sally must move to Florida for the winter so her brother doesn't get sick again. She meets a lot of new friends and has her daydreams to keep her occupied. But could the man in her building be Adolf Hitler?

5. **Byars, Betsy.** *The Not-Just-Anybody Family.* New York: Dell Publishing, 1986. 149 pages.

   This is the first book in a very humorous series based on the unusual Blossom family. The three young children live with grandpa, who is a real character, because mother is on the rodeo circuit. The zany adventures these children experience are very real and entertaining.

6. **Byars, Betsy.** *Wanted: Mud Blossom.* Illustrated by Jacqueline Rogers. New York: Dell Publishing, 1991. 148 pages.

   Scooty, the school hamster, is missing. Mad Mary's cane and bag are found on the side of the road. Is Pap's dog, Mud, responsible? Is that why he stays under the porch? And is someone out to murder Vern and Michael?

7. **Cleary, Beverly.** *Dear Mr. Henshaw.* New York: Dell Publishing, 1983. 133 pages.

   This is a story told through letters written to Mr. Henshaw, a writer, from Leigh Botts and a diary kept by Leigh. Leigh is trying to deal with the divorce of his parents and the absenteeism of his father. Leigh's mother is a caterer who is raising Leigh by herself and taking courses at the community college to become a nurse.

8. **Cleary, Beverly.** *Strider.* Illustrated by Paul O. Zelinsky. New York: Trumpet Club, 1991. 179 pages.

   The great sequel to *Dear Mr. Henshaw,* Beverly Cleary continues the adventures of Leigh Botts and his new dog, Strider. Both have had the feeling of abandonment but rise above it and become the best friends either one ever had. But can Strider really read?

9. **Conrad, Pam.** *Pedro's Journal.* New York: Scholastic, Inc., 1991. 80 pages.

   This is a journal of a young boy's adventures aboard Christopher Columbus's *Santa Maria.*

10. **Cooper, Susan.** *The Boggart.* New York: Scholastic, Inc., 1993. 196 pages.

    After visiting a castle inherited by her family, Emily and her brother discover they brought something back with them. What is it? And what will they do?

11. **Farmer, Nancy.** *Do You Know Me?* New York: Scholastic, Inc., 1993. 104 pages.

    Tapiwa's Uncle Zeka is visiting Zimbabwe. Tapiwa used to be bored, but her uncle is the most fun she has ever had. She hopes he will stay.

12. **Fleischman, Sid.** *The Whipping Boy.* Mahwah, NJ: Troll Associates, 1986. 89 pages.

    This is the story of Jemmy, the whipping boy, and Prince Brat. Jemmy must take any whippings for Prince Brat when the prince misbehaves, which is all the time. Together Prince Brat and Jemmy run away from the palace to start new lives. During their adventures, Jemmy and Prince Brat are taken by outlaws and rescued by Betsy and Petunia, the dancing bear.

13. **Gardiner, John Reynolds.** *Stone Fox.* New York: Trumpet Club, 1980. 81 pages.

    When his grandfather cannot pay his back taxes and risks losing his farm, Little Willy decides to spend his college money to enter a sled race. Willy later discovers that Stone Fox, an Indian, and his five Samoyeds have entered the race as well. They have never lost a race. Nevertheless Little Willy has his trusty dog Searchlight and he is determined to win.

14. **Haun, Mary Downing.** *The Doll in the Garden.* Boston: Houghton Mifflin, 1989. 128 pages.

After her father's death, Ashley and her mother rent a room in the house of Miss Cooper. Ashley later finds a doll in the garden with a note attached. Is the garden haunted by a young girl who died seventy years ago? And what does Miss Cooper have to do with it?

15. **MacLachlan, Patricia.** *Baby.* New York: Dell Publishing, 1993. 132 pages.

Larkin comes home to find a baby on her front porch with a note saying the baby's name is Sophie. Although unable to care for the baby now, the mother says she will be back for her someday. Sophie becomes one of the family. But what if the mother comes back? Will she take Sophie away?

16. **MacLachlan, Patricia.** *Journey.* New York: Dell Publishing, 1991. 83 pages.

Journey is left to stay with his grandparents after his mother's unexplained need to leave. She writes to them, but there is no return address. Journey searches to find the answers as to why his mother felt she had to leave and discovers much more.

17. **MacLachlan, Patricia.** *Sarah, Plain and Tall.* New York: Harper/Trophy, 1985. 58 pages.

Sarah moves to Kansas to be the wife of a widowed farmer and the mother of his children after answering the father's ad for a bride. Sarah changes the lives of this family for the better.

18. **Namioka, Lensey.** *Yang the Youngest and His Terrible Ear.* New York: Dell Publishing, 1992. 134 pages.

This is a wonderful story of friendship. Yingtao is the youngest in a family of musicians, except for Yingtao. After moving to Seattle, he finds a friend who helps him find something he loves and is good at. Now to tell his family.

19. **Naylor, Phyllis Reynolds.** *The Grand Escape.* Illustrated by Alan Daniel. New York: Dell Publishing, 1993. 148 pages.

Two house cats, Marco and Polo, make the grand escape into the unknown world. Ignorant of the dangers and ways of this new life, they are befriended by Carlotta and Texas Jake. The two cats soon learn that to join the Club of Mysteries with Carlotta and Jake, they must take some great risks.

20. **Naylor, Phyllis Reynolds.** *Shiloh.* New York: Dell Publishing, 1991. 144 pages.

When Marty discovers that Old Man Judd is abusing his dog, he decides he is going to buy, steal, or do anything to keep the dog safe from harm.

21. **Roberts, Willo Davis.** *The Girl with the Silver Eyes.* New York: Scholastic Inc., 1980. 198 pages.

Katie, by the sheer power of her mind, can move objects. She can also talk to animals, primarily cats. Unfortunately people are afraid of Katie. Her silver eyes make people uncomfortable. Katie finds out that there may be other children with her eyes and powers when she learns that her mother worked for a pharmaceutical company while she was pregnant working on a drug that had subsequently been taken off the market. At the time Katie's mother had worked for the drug company, so had three other women who all gave birth in the same month. Katie sets out to find the other three children.

22. **Sachar, Louis.** *There's a Boy in the Girls' Bathroom.* New York: Alfred A. Knopf, 1987. 195 pages.

Not only is Bradley the oldest fifth grader, he is the worst fifth grader ever. But the new school counselor sees a different side of Bradley. Will Bradley ever straighten up?

23. **Smith, Robert Kimmel.** *The War with Grandpa.* New York: Dell Publishing, 1984. 140 pages.

When Peter's grandmother dies, Peter's parents ask his grandfather to move in with them. Peter's grandfather, though, cannot climb the stairs to the guest room, so Peter is moved out of his room into the guest room. Peter is quite unhappy about this, and he decides to declare war on his grandfather. Initially Grandpa ignores Peter's attempt to start the war, but then he joins in the fighting until Peter does something that brings the war to a sudden end.

24. **Taylor, Mildred D.** *Roll of Thunder, Hear My Cry.* New York: Dell Publishing, 1976. 210 pages.

    An African-American girl is forced to learn the truth about life and what being black means.

25. **Wright, Betty Ren.** *The Doll House Murders.* New York: Scholastic Inc., 1983. 149 pages.

    Amy's Aunt Clare returns to the house where she grew up after being laid off from her job. One day when Amy is visiting her aunt, Clare offers to let Amy stay with her for a couple of weeks. Amy is at first unsure she will be able to stay because she must take care of her mentally handicapped sister, Louann, every day until her mother gets home from work. Her parents eventually allow her to stay. Once there, Amy discovers that the dollhouse in the attic, which had been given to her aunt on her sixteenth birthday, is haunted. She also learns that her aunt has carried a terrible memory with her for years.

Fifth Grade

1. **Alexander, Lloyd.** *The Book of Three.* New York: Dell Publishing, 1964. 224 pages.

   Join Taran, the assistant pig keeper, on his magical adventures to save his beloved Prydain. With the help of friends and determination, Taran is unstoppable.

2. **Babbitt, Natalie.** *Tuck Everlasting.* New York: Trumpet Club, 1975. 139 pages.

The Tuck family is no ordinary family, and something strange is going on behind their house. What is it, and will the Tucks be taken in by it?

3. **Cleary, Beverly.** *Ramona and Her Father.* New York: Avon Publishing, 1977. 186 pages.

    When Ramona's father loses his job, everyone is sad. Ramona does her best to cheer everyone up, but the more she tries, the more trouble she gets into. Ramona and her family get through it, and she learns something very important.

4. **Cooney, Caroline.** *The Face on the Milk Carton.* New York: Dell Publishing, 1990. 184 pages.

    One day Janie is forced to ask herself who she is, when she discovers her own face on a milk carton. If the Johnsons are not her real parents, who are? Was she kidnapped by the Johnsons?

5. **Cooney, Caroline.** *Whatever Happened to Janie?* New York: Dell Publishing, 1993. 199 pages.

    Janie discovers she was kidnapped, and her real parents want her back. Yet the Johnsons are not giving up. What will Janie (or is it Jennie) do?

6. **DeClements, Barthe.** *Nothing's Fair in Fifth Grade.* New York: Apple Paperbacks, 137 pages.

    Elsie, who is a bit overweight, is a new student in Mrs. Henson's fifth grade. At first none of the girls like her, and they discover she is stealing their lunch money. Later the girls find out why she is doing this, and they help her. Elsie tutors the other girls, and they become good friends. Elsie even begins to lose weight.

7. **Fox, Paula.** *Western Wind.* New York: Dell Publishing, 1993. 201 pages.

    Elizabeth feels her new brother is taking her parents away. She is to spend the summer with her grandmother. Even though she loves her grandmother, who is very understanding, she wants to be home. Then Elizabeth meets Aaron, and things begin to change.

8. **George, Jean Craighead.** *My Side of the Mountain.* New York: Trumpet Club, 1988. 177 pages.

Sam runs away from home into the Catskill Mountains. With only his wits, a few supplies, and information he read in a survival book, he sets out to live his own life. Will he stay there or come home?

9. **Konigsburg, E. L.** *From the Mixed-up Files of Mrs. Basil E. Frankweiler.* New York: Dell Publishing, 1967. 159 pages.

Tired of life at home, Claudia and her brother decide to run away and live in the Metropolitan Museum of Art. But just when they get comfortable, strange things start to happen. Told by Mrs. Frankweiler, this book is full of mysteries and surprises.

10. **L'Engle, Madeleine.** *A Wrinkle in Time.* New York: Dell Publishing, 1962. 190 pages.

Met and Charles Murray's father is missing. With the help of three very strange ladies, they set off on a strange and wild experience. How do these ladies know so much, and who is their father, anyway?

11. **Lisle, Janet Taylor.** *Afternoon of the Elves.* New York: Scholastic, Inc., 1989. 122 pages.

Sara-Kate doesn't fit in very well at school. Hillary likes her but is also a little unsure. Then the two girls discover an elf village in Sara-Kate's backyard. The elves teach the girls wonderful things.

12. **Lowry, Lois.** *Number the Stars.* New York: Dell Publishing, 1989. 137 pages.

Set in Denmark in 1943, this is the story of Annemarie and Ellen. Ellen is Jewish, and her family is facing "relocation" to a concentration camp. Annemarie's family must help Ellen's family make their way to freedom in Sweden.

13. **Naylor, Phyllis Reynolds.** *Night Cry.* New York: Dell Publishing, 1984. 154 pages.

After Ellen's brother is killed and another boy kidnapped, she wonders what is in the woods behind her house. Can Ellen uncover the secret of the woods and the night cries?

14. **O'Dell, Scott.** *Sing Down the Moon.* New York: Dell Publishing, 1970. 134 pages.

    Bright Morning and Running Bird must think fast before Spanish slavers threaten the peaceful valley. Will they escape this terrible fate?

15. **O'Dell, Scott, & Hall, Elizabeth.** *Thunder Rolling in the Mountains.* New York: Dell Publishing, 1992. 128 pages.

    In 1877, the miners came to the Wallowa River to pan for gold. Knowing they are outnumbered, a young Indian girl must come to grips with her life and what that means.

16. **Paterson, Katherine.** *Bridge to Terabithia.* New York: HarperCollins, 1987. 128 pages.

    Jess has been practicing all summer to be the fastest boy in the fifth grade. When a strange new girl decides to join the boys and beats Jess, he is bent on getting back at her. But he will never forget the friendship he finds with her at the bridge to Terabithia.

17. **Paterson, Katherine.** *Jacob, Have I Loved.* New York: Harper & Row, 1980. 175 pages.

    Louise is the healthier twin, but Caroline gets all the attention. Louise learns how to live as a waterman would. Watching Caroline get everything Louise dreamed of, Louise gathers her strength, accomplishes more than her sister ever could, and gains the respect of all.

18. **Paulsen, Gary.** *Canyons.* New York: Dell Publishing, 1990. 184 pages.

    Brennan Cole finds the 100-year-old skull of an Apache boy, Coyote Runs. Brennan finds an incredible journey ahead of him in his quest to return the skull to its rightful place.

19. **Paulsen, Gary.** *Hatchet.* New York: Trumpet Club, 1987. 195 pages.

On the way to see his father, Brian is in a plane crash in which the pilot dies. He is forced to live in the Canadian woods for 54 days with only a hatchet his mother gave him.

20. **Paulsen, Gary.** *The Haymeadow.* New York: Dell Publishing, 1992. 195 pages.

   John is forced to work the haymeadow all summer. He must tend to the sheep. But things start to go wrong for John. Is he strong enough to survive?

21. **Paulsen, Gary.** *The Winter Room.* New York: Dell Publishing, 1989. 103 pages.

   When Uncle David begins to tell stories, Eldon and Wayne listen anxiously. When Uncle David tells the story of the Woodcutter, things aren't the same.

22. **Peck, Richard.** *The Ghost Belonged to Me.* New York: Dell Publishing, 1975. 183 pages.

   After young Alexander discovers girls, he also discovers a ghost girl. He is blamed for things she does. What is he going to do?

23. **Savin, Marcia.** *The Moon Bridge.* New York: Scholastic, Inc., 1992. 231 pages.

   When Mitzi Fujimoto moves to San Francisco, she immediately becomes friends with Ruthie Fox. But when the U.S. government forces all Americans of Japanese ancestry to move to internment camps, Mitzi disappears. It is three long years before the friends are reunited.

24. **Spinelli, Jerry.** *Maniac Magee.* New York: HarperCollins, 1990. 184 pages.

   Wild stories are being spread about Jeffrey Magee. He's a legend in his town. When a real situation occurs, will Maniac Magee measure up?

25. **Winthrop, Elizabeth.** *The Castle in the Attic.* New York: Bantam Publishing, 1989. 179 pages.

   William's nanny is going home to England to be with her brother.

She gives William a toy castle that has been in her family for years. William does not want her to leave. Through the magic of the castle, William forces her to stay. But when he is forced to fight for her freedom and his, will he be brave enough?

Sixth Grade

1. **Avi.** *The True Confessions of Charlotte Doyle.* New York: Franklin Watts, 1990. 215 pages.

   A thirteen-year-old girl boards a ship and discovers she is the only passenger. She learns the captain is a murderer, but Charlotte is accused and convicted. Can she get out of it?

2. **Bunting, Eve.** *Sharing Susan.* New York: Harper/Trophy, 1991. 122 pages.

   At birth, two baby girls are mixed up and the parents take home the wrong child. This mistake is not discovered for twelve years. The problem is even more complicated because one child has died. Now the two sets of parents must decide how they are going to share Susan.

3. **Bunting, Eve.** *Sixth-Grade Sleepover.* San Diego: Harcourt Brace, 1986. 96 pages.

   The Rabbit Club is a group of avid sixth-grade readers. RABBITS stands for Read-A-Book: Bring-It-To-School. The Rabbit Club is having a sleepover in the school cafeteria, but Janey has a terrible secret—she is mortally afraid of the dark. Her parents work with the school to leave night lights on in the cafeteria and the restroom light shining into the cafeteria. Janey believes she can make it through the night, but she has a secret plan.

4. **Cushman, Karen.** *Catherine Called Birdy.* New York: HarperCollins, 1994. 212 pages.

   Catherine's father wants to marry her off to the richest suitor. She manages to dissuade several suitors. Then an ugly, old man comes to town. Unfortunately for Catherine, he is the richest suitor yet. Will she escape?

5. **Danziger, Paula.** *Not for a Billion Gazillion Dollars.* New York: Dell Publishing, 1992. 121 pages.

   Three teenagers create a business together to make a lot of money. Can they do it?

6. **Eckert, Allan W.** *Incident at Hawk's Hill.* New York: Bantam Publishing, 1987. 191 pages.

   This is a true story about an autistic boy who gets lost and is cared for by a mother badger who just lost her pups. Ben is able to communicate with the badger.

7. **Eisenberg, Lisa.** *Mystery at Bluff Point Dunes.* Mahwah, NJ: Troll Associates, 1990. 150 pages.

   Kate is staying with her good friend, Bonnie, on Cape Cod for the summer. Things start to disappear. When Kate begins to investigate, she may not want to accept what she finds.

8. **George, Jean Craighead.** *Julie of the Wolves.* New York: HarperCollins, 1992. 170 pages.

   Running away from an arranged marriage, thirteen-year-old Julie takes off to be with her friend in San Francisco. But she is lost in the Artic wilderness with no food or shelter. All seems lost until she wins over the affections of a wolf pack and the leader, Amaroq. With their help, she is able to eat, learns more about herself, and reflects on her life. She is later reunited with her father.

9. **Hamilton, Virginia.** *Anthony Burns: The Defeat and Triumph of a Fugitive Slave.* New York: Alfred A. Knopf, 1988. 193 pages.

   Anthony Burns is an escaped slave. After he is captured, he must await trial. Will Anthony ever be free?

10. **Hamilton, Virginia.** *M. C. Higgins, The Great.* New York: Macmillan, 1974. 278 pages.

    Two strangers are able to help M. C. live and realize his greatest dream.

11. **Hamilton, Virginia.** *Plain City.* New York: Scholastic Inc., 1993. 194 pages.

    When a girl discovers that what she knows about her father is all lies, her mother refuses to help her discover the truth. But she is determined to find out for herself.

12. **Lowry, Lois.** *Anastasia Krupnik.* Boston: Houghton Mifflin, 1979. 113 pages.

    Ten-year-old Anastasia's life is falling apart. Her parents are having a new baby, her teacher does not understand her, and the boy of her dreams does not know she is alive. But her secret green book helps her through it all.

13. **Lowry, Lois.** *The Giver.* New York: Dell Publishing, 1993. 180 pages.

    In a world where only the Giver possesses true feelings and emotions, Jonas finds he is next to possess this ability. Is her ready?

14. **Paterson, Katherine.** *Lyddie.* New York: Lodestar Books, 1991. 182 pages.

    Lyddie is a poor farm girl living in Virginia. She goes to Lowell, Massachusetts, to work in a factory. She gains her independence and fights for a better life for everyone.

15. **Paulsen, Gary.** *Island.* New York: Dell Publishing, 1988. 202 pages.

    When Will finds an island where he can be alone, he may never come back. Can Will face his fears or will he stay on the island?

16. **Paulsen, Gary.** *The River.* New York: Dell Publishing, 1991. 129 pages.

    The sequel to *Hatchet.* Brian is asked to go back to the situation he returned from. This time it is in a different place and with Derek. Derek is a man who is interested in teaching survival to others by observing how Brian was able to survive. But when things go wrong, can Brian bring them both back to safety?

17. **Peck, Robert Newton.** *Soup for President.* New York: Dell Publishing, 1978. 107 pages.

    This book takes place in Miss Kelly's class during the classroom elections for school president. Rob faces a dilemma when deciding who to vote for. His best friend, Soup, is running for the boys, and a girl he likes is running for the girls.

18. **Rawls, Wilson.** *Summer of the Monkeys.* New York: Dell Publishing, 1976. 283 pages.

    When Jay and his dog are out exploring, they discover a monkey in the middle of nowhere, and their summer becomes quite exciting.

19. **Rawls, Wilson.** *Where the Red Fern Grows.* New York: Dell Publishing, 1961. 249 pages.

    A young boy has two dogs who bring him more happiness and love than he ever dreamed of. In the end, however, all his love lies where the red fern grows.

20. **Roberts, Willo Davis.** *Baby-Sitting Is a Dangerous Job.* New York: Antheneum, 1985. 161 pages.

    Darcy has agreed to baby-sit Melissa, Jeremy, and Shana Foster. The three young children are ill behaved, though that is the least of Darcy's problems when one afternoon she and the three children are kidnapped. The kidnappers are the father and brothers of a girl Darcy knows from school. She knows that the man is violent because his daughter has run away several times to escape his abuse. Unfortunately Darcy lets the kidnappers know that she knows their names and thus puts her own life in danger.

21. **Sachs, Marilyn.** *A Pocket Full of Seeds.* New York: Scholastic Inc., 1973. 137 pages.

    Being Jewish in occupied France is not easy. Now Nicole and her family must find each other again and manage to survive.

22. **Selden, George.** *The Cricket in Times Square.* New York: Dell Publishing, 1960. 151 pages.

    A boy, a cricket, a mouse, and a cat become friends and overcome an obstacle that brings joy to a family in need.

23. **Speare, Elizabeth George.** *The Witch of Blackbird Pond.* New York: Dell Publishing, 1958. 249 pages.

    Moving from paradise to the bleak shore of Connecticut, Kit feels isolated in this new world. Befriending an old woman makes her feel less lonely, but it leads her to big trouble.

24. **Voight, Cynthia.** *Dicey's Song.* New York: Ballantine Books, 1982. 211 pages.

    Forced to hold her family together at the age of thirteen, Dicey grows up a little too fast. She finds it hard to live for herself and accept things from others. In the end, Dicey learns something very important.

25. **Yep, Laurence.** *Dragonwings.* New York: HarperCollins, 1975. 248 pages.

    Moon Shadow sails from China to visit the golden land where the father he has never seen lives. Although in a strange land, he comes to love his father and learns to live in this new world.

Appendix B: Glossary of Terms

Authentic Reading Assessment: Reading assessment that involves actual reading tasks in a natural environment such as a classroom; it should parallel regular instruction.

Cloze Passages: Refers to a reader's ability to identify missing letters to words or missing sections of a sentence.

Confirming: When a reader confirms a prediction about some aspect of a story or piece of text.

Demonstrations: The physical act of showing someone how to do something.

Environmental Print: Print that is used on signs, billboards, or consumer products.

Expository Text: Text that provides information to the reader; it may be organized in a variety of structures; most classroom textbooks are expository text.

Frustration Reading Level: The level at which a reader experiences extreme difficulty with decoding and/or comprehension.

Graphophonemic: The relationship between a written letter(s) of the English alphabet and the sound the letter (s) represents.

Hesitations: The pausing and stops a reader exhibits while oral reading.

Independent Reading Level: The level at which a reader can easily read materials without help from the teacher—little or no problem with decoding or comprehension.

Insertions: Words and phrases a reader adds to a text while reading.

Instructional Reading Level: The level at which a reader benefits from instruction regarding decoding and comprehension strategies; decoding and comprehension are still high.

Internalize: When the brain incorporates information in long term memory on a permanent basis.

Invented Spelling: Words that children spell as they write that are not conventionally spelled.

Miscue: Oral word errors that occur when a reader deviates from the printed text: examples include mispronunciations, substitutions, omissions, repetitions, and teacher-provided words.

Miscue Analysis: A systematic examination of a reader's oral word errors to determine what specific decoding strategies the reader employs when reading.

Narrative Text: Text that is organized around a story structure that includes character, setting, plot episodes, and resolution problems.

Personal Writing: Writing that may not be seen by other people (diary, journal, grocery list).

Predicting: Making a guess.

Prior Knowledge: The information a learner knows about a topic or subject before they read. Experiences a learner brings to an event.

Psychological Functions: Internal operations of the mind.

Reluctant Writers: Refers to learners who do not like to write or do not want to write because they lack self-confidence.

Representational Writing: Stories children write using strings of letters.

Retelling: A recounting of a story, in either written or oral form, after it has been read.

Sampling: Reading parts of a text, pausing to discuss or share the meaning of what was read.

Schemata: The collection of ideas and concepts that a person knows about any particular topic.

Scribble Writing: The marks children make when they start to write. The marks are not identified according to the standard alphabet.

Semantics: The prior knowledge and meaning a learner brings to any learning experience.

Syntax: Refers to the grammatical structures of a text.

Think Aloud: A strategy in which a reader is asked to talk about thoughts and ideas regarding a text during the reading act.

Traditional Reading Assessment: Typically, assessment in a multiple choice or simple answer format; most often requires literal knowledge and results in a numerical score.

Appendix C: How to Help Your Child Become a Better Writer

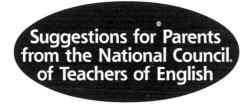

Suggestions for Parents from the National Council of Teachers of English

Dear Parent:

We're pleased you want to know how to help the NCTE effort to improve the writing of young people. Parents and teachers working together are the best means for assuring that children and youth will become skillful writers.

Because the situation in every home is different, we can't say when the best time is to pursue each of the following suggestions. In any case, please be aware that writing skill develops slowly. For some, it comes early; for others it comes late. Occasionally a child's skill may even seem to go backwards. Nonetheless, with your help and encouragement, the child will certainly progress.

The members of the National Council of Teachers of English welcome your involvement in your child's education in writing. We hope you will enjoy following these suggestions for helping your child become a better writer, both at home and at school.

Things to Do at Home

1. Build a climate of words at home. Go places and see things with your child, then talk about what has been seen, heard, smelled, tasted, touched. The basis of good writing is good talk, and younger children especially grow into stronger control of language when loving adults—particularly parents— share experiences and rich talk about those experiences.

2. Let children see you write often. You're both a model and a teacher. If children never see adults write, they gain an impression that writing occurs only at school. What you do is as important as what you say. Have children see you writing notes to friends, letters to business firms, perhaps stories to share with the children. From time to time, read aloud what you have written and ask your children their opinion of what you've said. If it's not perfect, so much the better. Making changes in what you write confirms for the child that revision is a natural part of writing—which it is.

3. Be as helpful as you can in helping children write. Talk through their ideas with them; help them discover what they want to say. When they ask for help with spelling, punctuation, and usage, supply that help. Your most effective role is not as a critic but as a helper. Rejoice in effort, delight in ideas, and resist the temptation to be critical.

4. Provide a suitable place for children to write. A quiet corner is best, the child's own place, if possible. If not, any flat surface with elbowroom, a comfortable chair, and a good light will do.

5. Give the child, and encourage others to give, the gifts associated with writing:

   - pens of several kinds
   - pencils of appropriate size and hardness
   - a desk lamp
   - pads of paper, stationery, envelopes—even stamps
   - a booklet for a diary or daily journal (Make sure that the booklet is the child's private property; when children want to share, they will.)

- a dictionary appropriate to the child's age and needs. (Most dictionary use is for checking spelling, but a good dictionary contains fascinating information on word origins, synonyms, pronunciation, and so forth.)
- a thesaurus for older children. (This will help in the search for the "right" word.)
- erasers or "white-out" liquid for correcting errors that the child wants to repair without rewriting

6. Encourage (but do not demand) frequent writing. Be patient with reluctance to write. "I have nothing to say" is a perfect excuse. Recognize that the desire to write is a sometime thing. There will be times when a child "burns" to write; others, when the need is cool. But frequency of writing is important to develop the habit of writing.

7. Praise the child's efforts at writing. Forget what happened to you in school and resist the tendency to focus on errors of spelling, punctuation, and other mechanical aspects of writing. Emphasize the child's successes. For every error the child makes, there are dozens of things he or she has done well.

8. Share letters from friends and relatives. Treat such letters as special events. Urge relatives and friends to write notes and letters to the child, no matter how brief. Writing is especially rewarding when the child gets a response. When thank-you notes are in order, after a holiday especially, sit with the child and write your own notes at the same time. Writing ten letters (for ten gifts) is a heavy burden for the child; space the work and be supportive.

9. Encourage the child to write for information, free samples, and travel brochures.

10. Be alert to occasions when the child can be involved in writing, for example, helping with grocery lists, adding notes at the end of parents' letters, sending holiday and birthday cards, taking down telephone messages, writing notes to friends, helping plan trips by writing for information, drafting notes to school for parental signature, writing notes to letter carriers and other service persons, and preparing invitations to family get-togethers. Writing for real purposes is rewarding, and the daily activities of families present many opportunities for purposeful writing. Involving your child may take some coaxing, but it will be worth your patient effort.

Things to Do for School Writing Programs

1. Ask to see the child's writing, either the writing brought home or the writing kept in folders at school. Encourage the use of writing folders, both at home and at school. Most writing should be kept, not thrown away. Folders are important means for helping both teachers and children see progress in writing skill.

2. Be affirmative about the child's efforts in school writing. Recognize that for every error a child makes, he or she does many things right. Applaud the good things you see. The willingness to write is fragile. Your optimistic attitude toward the child's efforts is vital to strengthening his or her writing habit.

3. Be primarily interested in the content, not the mechanics of expression. It's easy for many adults to spot misspellings, faulty word usage, and shaky punctuation. Perfection in these areas escapes most adults, so don't demand it of children. Sometimes teachers—for the same reason— will mark only a few mechanical errors, leaving others for another time. What matters most in writing is words, sentences, and ideas. Perfection in mechanics develops slowly. Be patient.

4. Find out if children are given writing instruction and practice in writing on a regular basis. Daily writing is the ideal; once a week is not often enough. If classes are too large in your school, understand that it may not be possible for teachers to provide as much writing practice as they or you would like. Insist on smaller classes—no more than 25 in elementary schools and no more than four classes of 25 for secondary school English teachers.

5. Ask if every teacher is involved in helping youngsters write better. Worksheets, blank-filling exercises. multiple-choice tests. and similar materials are sometimes used to avoid having children write. If children and youth are not being asked to write sentences and paragraphs about science, history, geography, and the other school subjects, they are not being helped to become better writers. All teachers have responsibility to help children improve their writing skills.

6. See if youngsters are being asked to write in a variety of forms (letters. essays, stories, etc.) for a variety of purposes (to inform, persuade. describe, etc.), and for a variety of audiences

(other students, teachers, friends. strangers, relatives, business firms). Each form, purpose, and audience demands differences of style, tone, approach, and choice of words. A wide variety of writing experiences is critical to developing effective writing.

7. Check to see if there is continuing contact with the imaginative writing of skilled authors. While it's true that we learn to write by writing, we also learn to write by reading. The works of talented authors should be studied not only for ideas but also for the writing skills involved. Good literature is an essential part of any effective writing program.

8. Watch out for "the grammar trap." Some people may try to persuade you that a full understanding of English grammar is needed before students can express themselves well. Some knowledge of grammar is useful, but too much time spent on study of grammar steals time from the study of writing. Time is much better spent in writing and conferring with the teacher or other students about each attempt to communicate in writing.

9. Encourage administrators to see that teachers of writing have plenty of supplies—writing paper, teaching materials, duplicating and copying machines, dictionaries, books about writing, and classroom libraries of good books.

10. Work through your PTA and your school board to make writing a high priority. Learn about writing and the ways youngsters learn to write. Encourage publication of good student writing in school newspapers, literary journals, local newspapers, and magazines. See that the high school's best writers are entered into the NCTE Achievement Awards in Writing Program, the Scholastic Writing Awards, or other writing contests. Let everyone know that writing matters to you.

By becoming an active participant in your child's education as a writer, you will serve not only your child but other children and youth as well. You have an important role to play, and we encourage your involvement.

Single copies of this statement are available free upon request, and may be copied without permission from NCTE. Multiple copies are available at a bulk rate of U.S. $7 per 100, prepaid only. Send request to NCTE Order Department, 1111 Kenyon Road, Urbana, IL 61801-1096.

Appendix D: National Council of Teachers of English Position Statement on Reading

Reading is the complex act of constructing meaning from print. We read in order to better understand ourselves, others, and the world around us; we use the knowledge we gain from reading to change the world in which we live.

Becoming a reader is a gradual process that begins with our first interactions with print. As children, there is no fixed point at which we suddenly become readers. Instead, all of us bring our understanding of spoken language, our knowledge of the world, and our experiences in it to make sense of what we read. We grow in our ability to comprehend and interpret a wide range of reading materials by making appropriate choices from among the extensive repertoire of skills and strategies that develop over time. These strategies include predicting, comprehension monitoring, phonemic awareness, critical thinking, decoding, using context, and making connections to what we already know.

As readers, we talk to others about what we are reading. These interactions expand and strengthen our comprehension and interpretation. In these interactions, we learn to read critically, to question what we read, and to respond in a certain way. We learn to ask:

- What is this text trying to do for me?
- Who benefits from this point of view?

These questions help us uncover underlying assumptions and motives that otherwise operate invisibly.

In order to make sure that all individuals have access to the personal pleasures and intellectual benefits of full literacy, NCTE believes that our society and our schools must provide students with

- access to a wide range of texts that mirror the range of students' abilities and interests;
- ample time to read a wide range of materials, from the very simple to the very challenging;
- teachers who help them develop an extensive repertoire of skills and strategies;
- opportunities to learn how reading, writing, speaking, and listening support each other; and
- access to the literacy skills needed in a technologically advanced society.

Furthermore, NCTE believes that . . .

- all teachers need to develop an extensive knowledge of language development, a thorough knowledge of all the language arts— including reading and a repertoire of teaching strategies deep and broad enough to meet the needs of every student;
- all administrators need to secure funds and provide opportunities for professional development; and
- all educational stakeholders—educators, policy makers, and the general public—need to understand that they can best support beginning and advanced readers by participating actively in public conversation about the broad goals of literacy learning while acknowledging teachers as curricula decision makers.

This position statement was adopted by the NCTE Executive Committee in February 1999. The Executive Committee at the time of adoption included the following members:

Joan Steiner
Jerome Harste
Anne Ruggles Gere
Sheridan Blau
Kathryn Egawa
Richard Luckert
Gwendolyn Henry
Yvonne Siu-Runyan
Charleen Silva Delfino
Elizabeth Close
Kathie Ramsey
Kathleen Blake Yancey
Nancy McCracken
Louann Reid
Victor Villanueva, Jr.
Pat Cordeiro
Ben Wiley
Keith Gilyard
Faith Schullstrom, Executive Director

Single copies of this statement are available free upon request, and may be copied without permission from NCTE. Multiple copies are available at a bulk rate of U.S. $7 per 100, prepaid only. Stock # 36516. Send request to NCTE Order Department, 1111 W. Kenyon Road, Urbana, IL 61801-1096.

References

Bialostok, S. (1992). *Raising readers: Helping your child to literacy.* Winnipeg: Peguis.

Bourgeois, P. (1989). *Grandma's secret.* Toronto, ON: Kids Can Press.

Bredekamp, S., & Copple, C. (1997). *Developmentally appropriate practice in early childhood programs: Serving children from birth through age 8.* Washington, DC: National Association for the Education of Young Children.

Bryson, B. (1990). *The mother tongue: English and how it got that way.* New York: W. Morrow and Co.

Goodman, Y. M., & Marek, A. M. (1996). *Retrospective miscue analysis: Revaluing readers and reading.* Katonah, NY: R. C. Owens.

Hill, M. W. (1989). *Home: Where reading and writing begin.* Portsmouth, NH: Heinemann.

Hydrick, J. (1996). *Parent's guide to literacy for the 21st century: Pre-K through grade 5.* Urbana, IL: National Council of Teachers of English.

Kropp, P. (1993). *The reading solution.* Toronto, ON: Random House.

MacBeth, A. (1989). *Involving parents: Effective parent-teacher relations.* Oxford, NH: Heinemann.

Milne, A. A. (1926). *Winnie-the-Pooh.* London: Methuen & Co., Ltd.

Murphy, J. (1993). What's in? What's out? American education in the nineties. *Phi Delta Kappan, 74,* 641–46.

Oglan, G. R. (1997). *Parents, learning, and whole language classrooms.* Urbana, IL: National Council of Teachers of English.

Penner, P.G., & McConnell, R.E. (1977). *Learning language.* Toronto, ON: MacMillan of Canada.

Peterson, R. (1992). *Life in a crowded place: Making a learning community.* Portsmouth, NH: Heinemann.

Phenix, J., & Scott-Dunne, D. (1991). *Spelling instruction that makes sense.* Markham, ON: Pembroke Publishers.

Rhodes, L. K., & Shanklin, N. L. (1993). *Windows into literacy.* Portsmouth, NH: Heinemann.

Smith, F. (1992). Learning to read: The never-ending debate. *Phi Delta Kappan,* February, 432–41.

Trelease, J. (1995). *The read-aloud handbook.* New York: Penguin.

Vygotsky, L. S. (1986). *Thought and language.* (A. Kozulin, Trans. and Ed.). Cambridge: MIT Press.

Vygotsky, L. S. (1978). *Mind in society: The development of higher psychological processes.* Cambridge: Harvard University Press.

Weaver, C. (1994). *Reading process and practice: From socio-psycholinguistics to whole language.* (2nd ed.). Portsmouth, NH: Heinemann.

Wells, G. (1986). *The meaning makers: Children learning language and using language to learn.* Portsmouth, NH: Heinemann.

G erry Oglan was born and raised in Windsor, Ontario, Canada, and has spent the last twenty years teaching for the Windsor Public Board of Education. He spent twelve of those years working with children with learning disabilities, and as a classroom teacher he taught grades 1 to 8. He also served three years as an assistant coordinator in charge of language arts programs for grades 4, 5, and 6. Four years ago he started working with parents because he was intrigued by the questions they asked about their children's education and its connection to their own educational histories. To help parents understand learning from a whole language perspective, he conducted evening sessions for parents and co-developed the Parent/Volunteer Inservice Program. He received his doctorate from the University of South Carolina in 1992 and is presently associate professor at Wayne State University in Detroit, Michigan. He lives in Tecumseh, Ontario, with his wife and two children.

Picture by Dan Reaume Photography

A veril Holton Elcombe was born in Windsor and went through the Windsor Public School system. Her first degree was from Hillsdale College In Michigan and she began her teaching career with severely emotionally disturbed preschool children in a Michigan hospital. Since then she has taught for twenty years in Ontario from JK to grade 8, including special education. For three years, she was a consultant for kindergarten and primary teachers with the Windsor Public Board and has given workshops to teachers, administrators, parents and graduate students in Ontario and Michigan. With Gerry, she developed the

Parent/Volunteer Inservice Program. She is currently a vice principal with the Greater Essex County District School Board. Her hobbies include photography, drawing, writing, and reading. Averil lives in Windsor, Ontario, with her husband, four daughters, dog, and cat in a house full of books.

*This book was typeset in Shannon by Electronic Imaging.
The typefaces used on the cover were Arial Black, Britannic Bold, and Times.
The book was printed on 60-lb. Lynx Opaque
by IPC Communication Services.*